LISTEN INNOVATE GROW

Michael Haynes & Garreth Chandler

Copyright © 2018

Michael Haynes & Garreth Chandler

Published in Australia by 2excell Consulting

National Library of Australia Cataloguing-in-Publication information available from nla.gov.au

ISBN: 978-0-646-98855-9 (paperback)

Printed in Australia

First Edition

Cover Design: Ikmah @ 99Designs

Interior Design & Layout: Swish Design

To my late mother, Phyllis Haynes, who taught me
the importance of hard work and tenacity necessary to
succeed in both business and in life!

CONTENTS

LISTEN INNOVATE GROW

Michael Haynes & Garreth Chandler

INTRODUCTION

Ryan Steyn started Empower Construction as a sole trader, supplying and installing external cladding for home builders. His aspirations for the business were high:

GOAL 1: $1million in revenue

GOAL 2: $1million in profit

10 YEAR GOAL: $100m in revenue, $10m in profits

Like many other SMEs, Empower Construction is good at what it does. Within three years of operation, they had established themselves as leaders in the residential cladding space.

That's when Ryan was confronted with the dilemma every SME owner faces when their business is going well:

How do you manage the growth needed to meet your financial targets without jeopardizing the ongoing viability of your business?

By taking a planned and structured approach to listening to and engaging with their customers, Ryan and his team saw the opportunity to expand Empower's offering to include rendering and painting.

The growth from these activities allowed the company to expand its operations and undertake new initiatives, including a more sophisticated marketing strategy that led to further growth.

As a result, Empower Construction has grown to more than 150 staff in just 11 years. It has received numerous accolades, and in 2017 Ryan was named the Optus Young Business Leader of the Year.

Best of all, the business is well on its way to achieving its ambitious ten-year target.

Why Business to Business (B2B) is the place to be

The B2B space is one that many SMEs are wary of playing in, as they may have previously struggled to:

- acquire and retain business customers (and so found it difficult to get off the ground)
- be profitable
- manage growth.

These challenges often result in SME owners and managers seeing B2B markets as 'too difficult' and 'not worth pursuing.'

That's a shame, because once you understand B2B markets and their key characteristics, you will see there are significant advantages to playing in that space.

Advantage 1: A smaller battlefield

Unlike consumer markets (B2C), there are fewer competitors in the B2B space. This makes it much easier to understand the strengths and weaknesses of each business. You can then:

- exploit their weaknesses, and gaps in their offerings
- use your company's strengths and capabilities to differentiate and compete more effectively.

It's often easier to have your company's message stand out and be heard in B2B than in B2C.

Advantage 2: Business customers tend to be loyal and 'sticky'

Once a business customer finds a product or service provider that meets their needs, they usually become very loyal. This can be attributed to factors including:

- The need to purchase the product or service in large quantities, making it difficult and/or impractical to change providers frequently
- The product or service serving an important purpose such as:
  - an input to production
  - meeting strategic objectives
  - ensuring the efficient operations of a business
  - resolving a specific problem.

That's why there's a mindset among business buyers to 'stick with who you know and what works.'

If you can meet your business customers' needs, they'll more than likely:

- Buy a large portion of the product or service from you (if not exclusively from you)
- Engage in long-term relationships and contracts with you, giving your company a constant and predictable revenue stream.

Why It's great to be an SME in B2B

The corporate world is increasingly recognizing the benefits of working with, and sourcing from, startups and SMEs including:

- Products and services better tailored to customer needs
- Higher levels of support
- Willingness to co-innovate
- Lower costs (often by using several smaller suppliers that want to retain control and are hungry for their business).

SMEs typically go above and beyond to meet their customers' needs, and their service level requirements often produce better quality outcomes at a lower cost.

Why we're passionate about this topic

In short, Garreth and I (Michael) are both SME owners servicing the B2B market.

Garreth is the founder and Managing Director of two successful SME businesses based in Australia. He has grown these companies from two-person operations to having more than 50 staff servicing clients in the UK, the US and Australia.

I've been working as an independent consultant specializing in B2B customer and marketing strategy for 12 years. I've also attended leading executive education programs and B2B conferences to stay on top of leading-edge approaches to building and growing B2B businesses.

Garreth and I have helped SMEs in countries including Australia, Canada and the USA grow and improve their business performance. We've worked with SMEs of all sizes—from sole trader (one-person) operations to SMEs with 250 staff across a variety of industries ranging from Human Resources and Law, to Information Technology and Automotive repairs.

In working with these companies, we've realized there's a lack of resources catering specifically to the start-up and SME tribe. Resources that provide clear and practical approaches for our tribe members to succeed in the world of B2B—one we believe presents enormous opportunities for startups and SMEs.

So *Listen, Innovate, Grow* has been written by us, for us.

Is this book for you?

Listen, Innovate, Grow is for people who are:

- Contemplating setting up a business that will operate in B2B markets (either partially or exclusively), and want to know how to achieve their growth ambitions
- Currently operating in B2B, and struggling to realize their growth ambitions

- In a growing B2B business and struggling to grow their business despite the market opportunities available.

This book is for anyone responsible for driving growth in their business such as:

- Founders and owners of startups and SMEs
- People in key leadership/strategic roles such as CEO, Managing Director and Head of Marketing/Strategy/Sales.

A new framework for SME B2B success

The key to unlocking your opportunities is knowing the dynamics of B2B and using a structured and strategic approach to achieve growth.

So we developed the *Listen, Innovate, Grow* B2B framework.

- **Listen** means getting an in-depth understanding of:
  - Your vision and goals
  - Your company
  - The market
  - Your customers (and prospects).

- **Innovate** is about the various ways SMEs can identify, prioritize and improve their business operations, products, services and marketing.
- **Grow** refers to how SMEs can proactively expand their operations, and manage their financials, people and company culture to sustain successful growth over the longer term.

This framework was developed from:

- Our two decades of experience working with a range of B2B companies and observing and recognizing their unique business challenges.
- In-depth interviews with business owners and managers of SMEs.

- Curating the best studies, papers and approaches developed to help people in this space.

By reading this book, you'll learn how listening, innovating and growing has allowed companies such as Empower Construction to overcome challenges and capitalize on the opportunities in B2B markets to achieve sustained growth and success.

How this book will work

Our book is structured around the Listen, Innovate, Grow (LIG) B2B Framework.

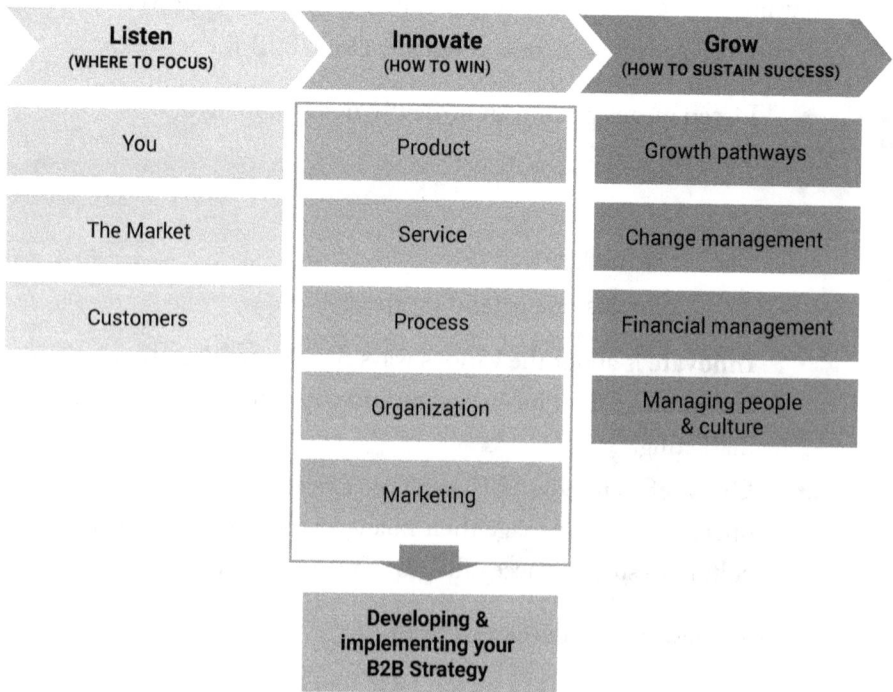

Listen (WHERE TO FOCUS)	Innovate (HOW TO WIN)	Grow (HOW TO SUSTAIN SUCCESS)
You	Product	Growth pathways
The Market	Service	Change management
Customers	Process	Financial management
	Organization	Managing people & culture
	Marketing	
	Developing & implementing your B2B Strategy	

The Listen, Innovate, Grow (LIG) B2B Framework

First, we'll show you who you should **listen** to when operating in B2B markets, and how to listen so you can plan the way forward for your company's growth.

Next, we'll teach you the four types of **innovation**, how to identify innovation opportunities, and how they can be applied in a SME B2B context.

Next, we'll discuss how to plan, implement and measure the success of your innovation endeavors.

Finally, we'll show you how to manage **growth** effectively.

At the end of each chapter we'll give you action items you can take on immediately as your business starts its growth journey.

At the end of the book you'll find a series of case studies profiling startup and SME companies from a range of industries, with the owners discussing their growth journeys and how they've applied the concepts of Listen, Innovate, Grow (LIG).

As you work your way through the book, we suggest you refer to the LIG diagram periodically to see how each step fits within the overall LIG approach. You may even want to print out the diagram and use it as a 'lens' to review your business as you apply the ideas and concepts in this book.

We also encourage you to visit **listeninnovategrow.com**, where you'll find further insights along with tools, templates and checklists to help you in your growth plans.

Now get ready to Listen, Innovate and Grow.

PART 1

LISTEN to know where to focus

Section overview

In this section, we talk about listening in a B2B context.

Listening in B2B happens at three levels:

- Listening to you, which means understanding your vision, aspirations, goals, key strengths, core capabilities and past performance
- Listening to the market, which means understanding current and emerging trends (industry, social, economic, technical), as well as competitor activities
- Listening to customers, which means understanding customer objectives, priorities, needs, pain points, buying behaviors and processes.

By listening (i.e. understanding and acknowledging the insights you gain from examining your company, the market and customers) you'll be able to develop a customer-driven strategy to drive the growth of your business.

In the next three chapters we'll explain how you listen to yourself, the market and your customers so you can develop successful strategies to drive growth.

CHAPTER 1

Listening to you

Chapter overview

'Listening to you' involves understanding why your business exists. This chapter is focused on defining your business in terms of:

- Mission
- Vision
- Goals

We'll help you develop a strong methodology to get feedback from internal channels, and ways to process that feedback.

Knowing what your company stands for

Our ultimate goal is to help you develop a growth strategy for your B2B SME. But before you can develop that strategy you need to understand:

- your company's mission
- what its vision is
- what its goals are.

Your Mission

Your company mission provides clarity on why your company exists and how it will serve its stakeholders, particularly its customers, employees and investors.

It is based on the values you want to create within the company. As an example, our mission at Evolve Research is to:

...use research to deliver business clarity and direction through innovative technology that brings data and customer understanding to life.

Your mission should be purposeful, succinct, easy-to-understand, and inspirational. Your employees and customers should be able to understand why you exist in just a few sentences.

Here are the missions of some other well-known B2B organizations. Although they're not SMEs, the examples are still illustrative:

***GE's** mission is to invent the next industrial era, to build, move, power and cure the world. ... In its labs and factories and on the ground with customers, GE is inventing the next industrial era to move, power, build and cure the world[1].*

*At **Microsoft**, our mission is to enable people and businesses throughout the world to realize their full potential[2].*

***SAP's** mission is to help every customer become a best-run business. We do this by delivering technology innovations that address the challenges of today and tomorrow without disrupting our customers' business operations[3].*

***Citi's** mission is to serve as a trusted partner to our clients by responsibly providing financial services that enable growth and economic progress. Our core activities are safeguarding assets, lending money, making payments and accessing the capital markets on behalf of our clients[4].*

These missions clearly set out the purpose of each company. However, they don't say how it will be done. That's important, because they shouldn't be restrictive. A mission should tell the reader *what* the company is trying to achieve, not *how* it is trying to achieve it.

It also communicates the *values* the company aspires to. Citi uses words such as 'progress', 'safeguarding' and 'trusted'. For Microsoft, the key word is 'enable'. These are important words that give the reader insight as to what the company truly believes in and aspires towards.

The company mission shouldn't be changed without careful consideration. However, missions *do* change over time as technology changes and companies adapt to meet the changing needs of their markets and customers. So it's important to review your mission periodically to ensure it's still relevant.

Your Vision

The vision of your company should be something *you* believe in and feel passionate about. It should explain why you started the business, and why you love doing what you do.

The company vision explains how you'll achieve your aims. This is important because it bridges the gap between aspiration and execution.

For example, Evolve Research's company vision is:

> *Our clients can trust and rely on the insights we deliver. We provide high 'return on investment' for our clients (saving them time and money). Our clients receive customized solutions, not one size fits all, and we have a genuine interest in the success of our clients. We don't just provide data, we provide direction[5].*

Here's Microsoft's company vision statement:

> *Microsoft is a technology company whose mission is to empower every person and every organization on the planet to achieve more. We strive to create local opportunity, growth, and impact in every country around the world[6].*

Here's an outtake from GE's company vision statement.

To become the world's premier digital industrial company ...

Transforming industry with software-defined machines and solutions that are connected, responsive and predictive ...

Executing critical outcomes for our customers[7] ...

You can see from these examples that the vision statement takes the mission to the next level by making it specific. It doesn't just say *what* the company stands for. It also says something about *how* it will be achieved.

Defining your Mission and Vision

If you don't have a mission, or you feel it's time to review the one you have, set aside a day to workshop it with your team. Getting them to buy into the mission by helping to define it is a worthwhile activity.

A lot of businesses develop a mission and a vision, but forget to share them with their employees and customers. If you haven't communicated your company mission and vision with your people, here are some ways you could do this:

- Display posters and other visual materials in the office that show your mission and goals.
- Link to them on your internet page and intranet site.
- Hold periodic internal workshops and fun, interactive sessions to motivate and inspire everyone to endorse and support the company mission and vision.

As well as having alignment at the founder and leadership level, it's important to communicate the company's mission and vision to staff at all levels of your company. This will ensure they all know what they're helping the company to achieve, and what's expected of them.

Tips for your mission and vision

- Be sure you clearly know your *Why*—the reason your business exists.
- Make your customers the hero, and keep your people focused on them. After all, they pay the bills.
- Keep it short, sharp and to the point.
- Don't be afraid to be aspirational. It's not so much about what you do now, but rather what you aspire to be.
- By all means, road test them with your people (e.g. team members and trusted colleagues) and customers. But don't get caught in the trap of designing mission and values by committee. Everyone will have their own ideas, and trying to include them all will lead to something that lacks clarity and purpose.
- Reinforce the mission and values periodically with both your customers and your employees.
- Ensure your marketing and communications remain consistent and aligned to your mission and values. A common mistake is to go off on a tangent when developing your marketing. Your marketing and branding collateral should always be anchored in your mission and values.
- Instill your vision and mission in company communications and take people on the journey. Reinforce where the business is heading and how it's progressing towards its goals.

Establishing your company goals

Mission and vision statements are intentionally non-specific. To translate these aspirations into how your company operates, you need to establish goals and lay down specific objectives your people can understand, plan for and work towards.

Before we talk about how this translation can occur, here's a reminder of a great business tool – the SMART acronym for goal setting[8].

Goal characteristic	What it means
Specific	The goal is precise, and doesn't leave any room for interpretation.
Measurable	The goal can be quantified so the outcome can be determined as either a success or a failure.
Attainable	The goal can realistically be achieved, as only achievable goals are motivating.
Relevant	The goal is aligned to the mission and values, and furthers the success of the company.
Timely	The goal will be completed within a specified time frame.

Applying this framework ensures the goals you set will actually benefit your business and help it achieve its mission.

Of course, you still need convert the high-level mission and values to a set of goals. A helpful business tool to establish and maintain your goals is McKinsey's *Three Horizons of Growth* framework[9], which defines three horizons:

- **Horizon one:** The core business activities, products and services that power cash flow and profit here and now. Goals at this level are about optimization and efficiency.
- **Horizon two:** These are emerging opportunities that will provide a pathway to growth but need 'considerable investment' to achieve.
- **Horizon three:** These are ideas that *could have* merit in future. They're more speculative, but reviewing and assessing them early means mitigating future risks.

You need to define goals at each horizon that take the form of developing projects, capabilities, improvements and initiatives (innovations) that will power the growth of your business.

In the context of this book, the *Three Horizons of Growth* framework gives you a way to develop goals in your planning cycle that ensures your company is forward looking, without neglecting the core business areas that generate cash flow today.

Who do we mean by 'you'?

In other words, who and what should you listen to?

1. Your people

While a key focus of this book is listening to and learning from customers, you shouldn't forget one of your business' key resources—your own people.

Listening to your people will benefit them as much as it will you. Having your thoughts and ideas heard encourages a sense of participation and contribution. Listening to your people gives them a sense of ownership of the company goals which is exactly what you want, because people who feel ownership of the company goals are more likely to complete them.

Of course, you'll need to manage expectations. But we're yet to find a business where the employees didn't love being asked what they thought.

Here are some other reasons why you should listen to your employees:

- **They know more about your business than anyone else** because they work in (and on) it every day. The people who operate within the business and deliver the products and services of your company have a wealth of information and insights about what works and what doesn't.

- **Your frontline service people spend a lot of time with your customers.** As a result, they know where you deliver well and where you need to, and can, improve. Chances are, they're also strong advocates who'll see the customers' point of view and act as their representatives when it comes to working on internal projects to develop new products and services.

- Your **sales people** understand how to compete with other providers in the market. They know which competitors do things well, and which ones don't. Their commercially-focused point of view will give you a reality check on whether ideas have commercial merit and help you compete or develop new revenue opportunities.

You should also listen to your **suppliers and partners**. Ask them how much they like working with you and where you can improve. They have the benefit of working with lots of customers, some of whom will likely be your competitors. Of course, they'll be limited by Commercial in Confidence agreements on what they can say. But it doesn't hurt to ask, and it's in their best interest to help you succeed by providing constructive feedback.

Key questions to ask your people:

- Do you understand what we do? Why we are here?
- Do you think we achieve it – always, sometimes, never?
- In the instances where we don't, why not?
- What are our strengths? Where do we perform best? Why?
- Who else provides the services we provide?
- What do they do well and why?
- If they do better than us, why is that? Specifically, what do they do better?
- Where do we do better than them? Why?
- If you could focus on three areas we could do better and make the biggest difference, what would they be?

2. Your financial reporting

Later in the book we'll review financial management for growth companies in detail. But at this stage we'll just say that you need to listen to your financial reporting to understand how well you're addressing your mission, and where the threats and opportunities lie.

With the right cost accounting system in place, you should be able to monitor and understand:

- Where the **bulk of your revenue is earned,** and therefore where you should invest your cash flow to develop further capability to maintain your success.
- Where you're **spending your capital**. Don't forget to look at profit as well as income. It's no good having high sales if most of the income is chewed up by costs and overheads. You should have a strong understanding of the relationship between spend and return in the business.
- Where you're **growing revenue** quickly in terms of product lines, types of customers or new line or product extensions. Being able to quickly spot where you're getting traction means you can review your priorities and, if necessary, focus on and invest in the high-growth parts of your business.
- **Where revenue is declining or stagnant**. This gives you a starting point for asking questions about why you aren't growing. It can help you determine whether it's due to a market shift, or whether your business isn't competing effectively due to a deficiency in how you've developed, marketed or positioned a product to customers.

These questions naturally lead to the *Three Horizons of Growth* framework by showing where you need to prioritize innovation to improve your operational capabilities—both current and future. It also serves as protection against rapid obsolescence.

3. Your other non-financial operational indicators

While financial indicators are a great way to listen to your business, they're what we call **lag indicators**. They're the results you get from executing an operational strategy. But it's better to address an operational issue *before* it affects your financials, not *after*.

To do this, you need good **lead indicators**, such as:

- volume of customer enquiries, ideally categorized by topic
- customer complaints
- technical support logs
- customer feedback from tenders
- internal metrics such as lead time for deliveries, order volumes, and data on enquiry types.

4. Your capabilities and resources

The final way to 'listen to you' is to review and understand your **company's capabilities**. Think of this as a stocktake of the resources and capabilities your company has to deliver on its mission and vision. It will help you identify any capability gaps that will prevent you from achieving your goals, mission and vision.

Here's what you should focus on as part of your capability review:

- **Finances:** Do you have the money to achieve your goals? That is, do you have enough capital and cash flow to fund the activities you defined in your planning? Your budgeting process should be mature enough to estimate the costs of different innovation activities in terms of:
  - the amount of resources they tie up
  - any direct costs they create where money is spent on outside consultants, products or services.

- **Equipment:** Does your business have the tools to deliver? For example, if you're a commercial real estate agent and want to create a new way for buyers to find property, do you have the technology platform you need to do it? Can your database capture and retain property details and push them to potential new buyers, or do you need to invest in that capability?

Or perhaps you're a packaging manufacturer looking to create a new way to package small perishable goods. Can your manufacturing equipment be retooled to produce the product? Or will you need to invest in new equipment?

- **Staff:** Do you have enough people to achieve your objectives? If you bring in new people, what are the implications for your profitability? If you re-deploy the people you have, how will it affect the projects or 'business as usual' activities they were working on?

- **Skills and expertise:** Do you have people on board with the knowhow you need to achieve your goals? This can be broken down into three groups:

  - managerial and project management focus
  - subject matter expertise to develop the capability
  - sales and marketing focus and expertise—moving forward to commercialize your offerings.

  If you have gaps in any of these areas, you'll need to consider bringing people in to fill the gaps through re-deployment or hiring new staff.

- **Methodologies:** Do you have the processes to innovate successfully? You might use:

  - a formal 'go to market' process
  - project management disciplines such as Six Sigma
  - agile methodologies.

How and when to listen to 'you'

Listening to your people, your customers, other stakeholders and financial results ultimately tells you whether you're achieving your mission and vision. Missions and Visions often end up as wallpaper—nice words that don't have any direct connection to the way you run your business day to day. In this sense, listening means asking the following questions again and again:

- **"Is our business doing the right thing?"** Is your mission relevant to the market you serve, and will your vision get you there?
- **"Are we delivering successfully?"** Do you need to change what you're doing? If the market or your company has moved over time, do you need to set a new mission and vision? There's nothing inherently wrong with changing your mission and strategy, but are you sure it's the right thing to do? Are you achieving the goals you defined in your planning cycle?
- **"Is the business still working for me?"** Do you feel a sense of purpose, belonging, motivation and reward while working in the business? Even if you answered "Yes" to the first two questions, do you still feel motivated and involved?

Most businesses work on an annual cycle with quarterly reviews. In our experience this is an appropriate frequency. Reviews need to be frequent enough to understand progress and remediate any issues preventing progress without wasting everyone's time because little has changed or been accomplished.

But you don't have to wait until your next management meeting to 'listen to you'. You can (and should) create other listening opportunities.

Channels for listening to you

- **Establish cross-functional groups** to focus on projects at each horizon. Involve people from both the front line and back of house.
- **Run internal focus groups.** Set up forums to focus on specific goals and review progress in a more intensive session.
- **Run an internal online community.** Set up a form on your intranet, or use other business social platforms that focus on innovation and innovation projects, to deliver your growth ambitions.
- **Have quarterly forums with staff.** Let your people turn off their devices and take time out of the business so they can focus on reviewing it. Having a dedicated 'time out' means people will be focused on how the business is doing, and you can get them involved in becoming part of initiatives to drive future growth.
- **Run a regular employee survey.** Most businesses run employee satisfaction or engagement surveys. But there's nothing stopping you from using these surveys to collect feedback and ideas about innovation, and to listen to the thoughts and ideas of your people. One benefit of this approach is you can use survey methods to quantify results (i.e. have people rate the potential impact of different potential opportunities as areas of future focus).

Chapter summary

In this section we reviewed what it means to 'listen to you', starting with the idea of setting a company mission and vision. From there we looked at how to set goals based on the mission and vision (which are aligned to growth) using McKinsey's *Three Horizons of Growth* framework. We also talked about the importance of making these goals SMART.

We then discussed how 'listening to you' means engaging with your people to unlock their knowledge and understanding of your company. This ultimately helps you determine whether your company is on track to achieving its goals by being clear about its capabilities in three areas—finances, people and resources.

....

Take action now

- Review your company mission and values to ensure they're relevant and communicated to your team.
- Establish a regular process to establish, review and assess the achievement of goals aligned to the mission and values.
- Define your feedback channels to determine if, how and why you are getting there.
- Review your capabilities to understand any gaps preventing your company from achieving its goals.

We'll now switch from 'listening to you' to 'listening to the market', another critical piece of the puzzle that will inform your growth strategy.

CHAPTER 2

Listening to the market

Chapter overview

In this chapter we'll discuss how to analyze and gain an in-depth understanding of B2B markets—particularly those your business operates in. By 'listening to the market' you'll be able to determine the attractiveness of those industries and markets, and identify opportunities and threats. This will allow you to determine which markets you should pursue as part of your company's growth strategy.

What does 'listening to the market' mean?

Listening to the market is about knowing which industries and geographies you should focus on in your B2B customer-driven strategy. You find out 'where to play' by learning about the characteristics and dynamics of the industries and markets your company is pursuing—both current and prospective.

You do this by 'listening' to them, and learning about their:

- market performance
- trends
- competitors

Understanding market performance

To understand their market performance, you need to understand how both the industries and geographies you currently operate in (or want to) are performing. Are they growing, shrinking or stable? And what revenues and profits are they generating?

Answering these questions will help you determine whether or not a market is a potential growth opportunity.

Here are some key metrics you should examine (in both absolute terms and growth rates) as part of your market assessment:

- Number of businesses operating
- Number of businesses that have entered
- Number of businesses that have exited
- Revenues
- Profits Generated

Understanding market trends

You also need to understand trends that could be affecting the industries and markets your company will be pursuing. These trends, which may vary depending on the industries, can include:

- **Industry economics:** Industry-wide factors such as costs for key supplies, equipment and transport could affect the viability and profitability of operating in some industries.
- **New technologies:** Incumbents in the industry may be using new technologies to either provide additional value or improve service to customers or to generate cost savings and efficiencies within their own companies. Alternatively, end customers (i.e. your customers' customers) may be using new technologies.
- **Legal/regulatory changes:** Providers could face requirements such as obtaining certifications or meeting requirements in terms of service levels, safety, types of equipment and/or inputs used.

These could have implications for your business in terms of cost and staffing, which may affect the attractiveness, viability and profitability of operating in that industry.

- **Customer trends:** These can occur on two levels.

  1. The business customers you're potentially targeting may change their behaviors, requirements and preferences. For instance, business buyers in the professional services market are increasingly opting to use niche, specialist firms and individuals to complete work instead of large, generalist 'big name' firms. Such changes in B2B customers could present opportunities for your company to provide new offerings and/ or change and enhance existing ones.

  2. Changes to the end customer's behavior, requirements and preferences may affect the industry's attractiveness and potential for opportunities. It could also affect what products and services your company needs to provide to remain relevant in that industry. For example, with the number of home-based office workers in markets such as Australia expected to increase to 60%, office fit-out suppliers and design companies must ensure they have the appropriate product mix to meet this emerging end-user trend.

- **Consolidations and mergers:** It's important to determine whether there are significant company-consolidations, mergers and acquisitions occurring in:

  - the industries you are targeting
  - the companies involved
  - the driving forces behind them.

This will allow you to not only determine the industry attractiveness, but also understand the competitive landscape in terms of:

  - the number of companies that will remain as potential customers

- the products and services your company may need to provide to meet the needs of these merged entities.

- **Adjacent industries and markets:** It's also important to understand the customer trends, innovations and technologies occurring in other industries. It can help you identify opportunities your company can pursue within its target industries and markets.

Understanding your competitors

A third market component you must listen to is your competitors. Even if market performance and trends seem attractive, the competitive activity can determine whether you'll pursue certain markets, and how you'll compete and operate within them.

Competitor analysis will allow you to:

- identify your key competitors
- understand their strategies
- understand their strengths and weaknesses relative to the products and services your company provides.

And with this knowledge you'll be able to:

- identify gaps and weaknesses in competitor offerings
- identify opportunities for your company to:
  - develop new products and services
  - enhance your existing product and service offerings
  - discover new market trends.

Understanding your competitors will help you determine the markets and customers you should focus on, and how your company will differentiate itself and stand out from the competition.

How to undertake a B2B competitor analysis

When undertaking a B2B competitor analysis, make sure it's a buyer-driven approach. (This point is often overlooked.) This means your analysis must reflect the alternatives that buyers and their influencers within a particular industry would consider.

Buyers and influencers will consider multiple options to meet their objectives and requirements. They may look at either:

- direct competitors with similar product or service offerings
- indirect competitors with different product or service offerings that still give them what they want.

For instance, an IT company looking for marketing support may either consider marketing agencies or hire an independent marketing consultant through a talent platform such as Freelancer.com or Expert 360 to provide marketing support.

Ensure you create a buyer-driven competitor list

As you compile your list of competitors to analyze, make sure it's created from a buyer point of view. A study conducted by the Rain Group found there's only a 25% overlap in the competitor lists between buyers and sellers[10].

You can avoid this trap and create a buyer-driven competitor list by:

- using some of the research sources we talk about later in the chapter
- speaking with current and prospective customers (something we'll discuss in the next chapter).

What to include in your B2B competitor analysis

Your competitor analysis should look at the following:

WHAT ARE THEIR OBJECTIVES?

- What is their Company Mission and Vision?
- What are their financial and/or strategic objectives?

Insight gained: Where they're focused, what they might do next, and how your company should respond.

WHAT ARE THEIR STRATEGIES?

- What markets and customers do they currently focus on?
- What's their strategic direction moving forward?
- What is their value proposition?
- What is their basis of differentiation?

Insight gained: What their focus is now, basis of competition, and indications as to their future directions and areas of focus.

WHAT ARE THEIR CAPABILITIES AND RESOURCES?

- What do these companies have in terms of:
  - resources (e.g. funding, equipment, staff)?
  - capabilities (e.g. skills, expertise, methodologies)?

Insight gained: Your competitors' weaknesses, skills, capabilities and resources, which could be strong indicators of what your company needs to compete effectively.

WHAT DO THEY DELIVER?

- What products and services do they offer?
  - What are their core offerings? What do they offer to provide additional value?

- What do they offer their buyers specifically to help meet their broader strategic, financial and personal objectives?

Insight gained: Opportunities to differentiate by expanding and/or improving your current product and service offering.

HOW DO THEY DELIVER?

- How do they provide their products and services?
  - What channels do they use?
  - What customer experience do they give?
  - How do they service and support their customers (e.g. online, face-to-face, via partnerships, peer-to-peer/self-service)?
  - How do they collaborate and work with their customers?
  - What service levels/service guarantees do they provide?

Insight gained: Opportunities to differentiate by changing and/or enhancing the service, support and customer experience provided.

HOW DO THEY PROMOTE TO AND ENGAGE WITH CUSTOMERS?

- What mechanisms do they use to promote and engage with customers? What approaches do they use to promote and engage specifically with decision makers? Do they use:
  - social media?
  - events (e.g. workshops, forums, seminars, webinars)?
  - thought leadership (e.g. blogs, videos, podcasts, white papers)?
  - case studies?
  - awards and accreditations/certifications?
  - customer reference programs?

Insight gained: How to improve and differentiate how you engage with current customers and attract and acquire new ones.

Sources for market and competitor information

Here are some ways to get an understanding of the industries and markets you operate in, and the competitors you're up against.

- **Competitor websites:** These often contain a lot of information about their products and services. Larger organizations often include annual reports and company presentations, which can provide insights into their strategies, capabilities and future directions.

- **Consulting firm industry reports:** Global consulting firms such as Bain, McKinsey, Accenture and PWC often produce detailed reports about industry performance and trends, which they then make available on their website for a fee (if not for free).

- **Syndicated market research reports:** These reports produced by specialist research firms such as IBISWorld, Forrester and Gartner provide detailed analysis and facts for industries. (In most cases there's a fee involved.)

- **Industry and professional associations:** These associations often produce reports, and host events covering industry trends and topics.

- **Government department industry reports:** These are available from relevant federal government departments such as the Australian Bureau Statistics and Statistics Canada.

- **Social media:** You can get some good insights into your competitors' intentions and areas of focus from their LinkedIn and Twitter accounts.

- **Mystery shopping:** Having your employees pose as potential customers can give you an insight on the service and customer experience/customer engagement your competitors offer.

- **Decision maker summits:** Also known as roundtables or forums, these invitation-only events are organized to discuss the issues, challenges and aspirations important to decision makers. B2B companies typically use summits to understand their customers and prospects, and build strong relationships with them. I'll be discussing them in more detail in the next chapter, but I'm mentioning them now because they can be a good way to learn about market challenges and trends.

Chapter summary

Listening to the market by undertaking market and competitor analyses is critical to learning about the industries and geographies your company operates in. Conducting your competitor analysis using a buyer-driven approach will give you a thorough understanding of the competitive landscape and help you determine:

- appropriate market opportunities for your company
- how your company should position and differentiate itself to penetrate and grow in a particular market.

Take action now

Get together with your management team and ask the following questions:

- Who are our competitors?
- Would our current customers and prospects think of them as alternatives? How do we know? Are there any others we should consider?
- How do our customers and prospects compare alternative offerings and solutions?
- When was the last market and competitor analysis update? When is the next one due?
- Can we answer all the questions and topics outlined in this chapter? How can we fill the gaps?

CHAPTER 3

Listening to your customers

Chapter overview

In this chapter, we'll be discussing how you listen to business customers. That is, how to learn about their priorities, objectives, needs and behaviors.

The B2B buying process often involves a number of stakeholders, so we'll begin by talking about:

- who these key players are
- what their roles are in the buying process
- what you need to know about each of them
- the best way to listen to them.

By getting to know your customers, your company becomes a customer-driven company, which will allow you to achieve the growth you want.

Understanding the key players in the B2B buying process

Learning about the customers you want is the key to acquiring and retaining business customers, and ultimately growing your business.

Understanding your business customers is all about knowing about the main participants in the B2B buying process.

According to studies by the Corporate Executive Board, on average about 6.8 people are involved in a purchase decision.[11]

The main participants in the buying process are:

- decision-makers
- executive buyers
- internal influencers
- change agents
- corporate sourcing (procurement)
- users
- blockers

The first four (decision-makers, buyers, influencers and change agents) are often referred to as the buying group. They're often the primary participants in purchases that have significant financial and/or strategic implications.

Decision-makers (the real buyers)

In terms of a specific purchase, the decision-makers are usually a few members of senior management. In small and medium-sized companies, it may just be just the business owner. The decision-makers do the deals and make the actual purchasing decisions. Hence, they ultimately determine whether your company will do (or continue to do) business with their company.

That said, in many organizations the true buyer may not use, be involved with or even be familiar with the details of your product or service offering. They'll be more focused on:

- achieving broader strategic objectives
- meeting their own personal agendas
- ensuring due diligence has been undertaken.

This means they'll listen to the recommendations of influencers, who we'll talk about shortly.

Executive buyers

The leadership team of the B2B companies you want to service is often referred to as the executive buyer. They're often the true buyers because they base their final decision on their own personal objectives.

So when you engage with the executive buyer it's important to understand:

- their broader strategic objectives and priorities
- their key challenges
- industry trends
- their own personal agendas, which may involve seeking a promotion or a new role within their industry.

Armed with this deeper understanding, you can help executive buyers achieve their goals and 'look good' by delivering what they need, whether it's:

- strategic advice
- tailored products and services
- access to subject matter experts or industry leaders
- opportunities to engage with industry peers.

By meeting their broader needs, they'll see your company as a trusted partner and advisor, and you'll be able to develop a long-term relationship with them as a customer. Not only will they keep buying from you, they'll also work with you to create new offerings and even provide referrals and recommendations as your company's advocate.

Internal influencers

Internal influencers affect B2B purchase decisions because they have an important say. They often set buying specifications, provide information, evaluate alternatives, and recommend a particular solution and supplier for the company.

This can be a rather straightforward process. But if you're offering a complex product or service that affects different parts of the organization, there may end up being a large number of internal influencers (ie. stakeholders) who have a say in the purchasing decision. Influencers can come from departments such as finance, IT, marketing and engineering. Some end users may also become internal influencers who also have a say in the selection process.

Change agents (your secret weapon)

Change agents are great at building consensus among their colleagues and decision-makers. Getting that consensus is a major challenge for B2B product and service providers, which is why you need to identify change agents in the companies you want to win business with as early on in the process as possible.

Change agents are highly respected and well-regarded by both management and staff. They won't have a particular role or title, and probably won't be a senior executive. But chances are they:

- have researched and understand the alternatives to your product or service
- are often looked upon during meetings to answer questions and/ or provide their perspective
- ask very advanced and knowledgeable questions
- drive change across the organization
- are often emotionally attached to solving the problem and selecting the best product or service provider for their company
- understand the company politics and how things *really* get done, including who the buyers are and how they actually buy. This knowledge is often referred to as the **informal organization**[12].

To get your company's product or service offering into an organization—particularly a larger and more complex one—you must identify a change agent who will:

- give you an understanding of the company's informal organization
- help mobilize, build consensus, and convince the decision makers to buy from you.

Identifying a company's change agent isn't easy. You'll need to do some research and use your business contacts to identify an appropriate person to be an effective change agent on your company's behalf.

Here are some characteristics to look for in a potential change agent/mobilizer:

- They talk about needs and challenges in terms of the group, department or company (as opposed to just their individual needs.)
- They engage with (and possibly challenge) thought-provoking insights you bring to their attention, such as those pertaining to relevant industries and market trends.
- They follow through on the requests you make, such as:
  - setting up a meeting with specific attendees
  - researching something that's happening in their organization and providing their point of view.

Once you've found a change agent, the key to getting them to help you understand the informal organization is to build trust and demonstrate value.

You create value by providing insights that:

- teach them something new and compelling about their business and its challenges
- outline why the company's current ways of operating could be costing the business time, money or lost opportunities
- explain the benefits of taking action (and the costs of inaction)[13].

Always keep in mind what you're trying to do: to get them publicly advocating for change in the company, and recommending your company's product or service offering. Their desire for change will be driven far more by the personal value of your insights than by the business value to their organization. So as you engage with the change agent, think about how the insights and information you provide could help them in advancing their career or being perceived as a better leader.

One more thing: Change agents tend to change jobs frequently because they get bored and look for new challenges and ways to make an impact. This can be great for your company, because if you help them in one organization, they'll recommend your products or services at their next organization.

Corporate sourcing (procurement)

Purchases are often the responsibility of a purchasing or procurement department, particularly repeat purchases. They also often rely on 'preferred supplier' lists.

With large companies focusing more and more on cost management, the influence of this type of buyer is increasing. You usually find them in companies where the function is centralized and they're given authority at a stipulated regional, divisional or HQ level.

If your company has to deal with corporate sourcing as part of your selling process (if you haven't already, you will at some point), here's what we suggest:

- Make sure you have an in-depth understanding of your customers' and prospects business, including their key objectives and their strategic and financial priorities. It will help you position your company's offerings and the benefits and value they'll create.
- Have customer plans for your key customers and prospects so you can manage the entire customer relationship across all stakeholders and avoid any purchasing conflicts. (We'll talk about creating B2B customer plans later in this book.)

Users

As the name implies, these are the people who use the product and/or services. Depending on the organization, they:

- may not have any impact on the purchasing decision process
- may have requested the product, and be on the path to becoming a change agent
- could potentially serve as an influencer.

Blockers

Blockers are customer stakeholders who try to prevent a supplier from closing a deal. They may:

- dislike the supplier
- prefer a competing supplier
- want to maintain the status quo.

You can find blockers at any level of the organization and in any buying role, and their influence can vary.

Blockers can also be deceptive. They may appear supportive during meetings with you and their peers, but then sabotage any chance of your company being selected behind the scenes.

The best way to address blockers is to:

- identify who they are by consulting with other stakeholders—most likely a change agent or influencer advocating for your product
- determine whether they can be persuaded by the change agent and other stakeholders in the group.

If they can be persuaded, you can:

- identify influencers the blocker respects, and have your change agent facilitate a discussion between them

- conduct a workshop or meeting where the stakeholders and the blocker can exchange views
- supply the change agent and other influencers with information to convince the blocker to support the deal
- listen to and empathize with the blocker's concern regarding change. If possible, connect them with current or previous customers who had similar concerns.

Understanding the needs of buyers and users

To acquire and retain business customers, and ultimately grow your business, you must meet their needs by delivering value. To do that, you need to focus on:

- what you deliver (i.e. your company's offerings)
- how you deliver (i.e. processes, service and service levels) in line with their needs.

But remember, when it comes to B2B markets (particularly in larger companies), buyers and users each have their own distinct requirements. Satisfying the user's needs only could cost your company business because the buyers may not realize your company is fully capable of meeting their needs too.

The table on the next page is a summary of the priorities of buyers and users, and how to deliver on the needs of both parties:

Customer role	Priorities	What you must deliver	How you must deliver
Buyers (Decision-Makers, Influencers, Change Agents)	Identifying opportunities Responding to threats and trends Sustaining profitable growth Positioning themselves and company as the market leaders Helping to work through overarching strategies and plans	Insights such as industry trends and developments Advice on addressing strategic objectives and challenges Identification of opportunities	Thought leadership Strategic dialogue including: • Industry/peer engagement • Customer engagement
Users	Product features Capabilities and functional areas of expertise Industry specialization and experience Achievement of stipulated KPIs, deadlines, milestones and performance levels	Tailored products and solutions Required functionalities Specific capabilities Value added services (e.g. training, reporting) Industry expertise	Service levels (e.g. hours of operation, service delivery methods) Service guarantees Easy customer service and buying processes Market reach

By delivering to the needs of both buyers and users, your company will go from being a reliable supplier that meets the needs of its users to being a trusted partner and advisor. You'll keep your customers longer, secure more of their business, and even become their exclusive supplier.

As you earn more trust from decision-makers, they'll be more likely to provide referrals and pay a premium for your company's solutions. This can lead to higher margins, which will in turn help your company pursue profitable growth.

The B2B buying process isn't static. It varies according to each company and the type of purchasing involved.

In some instances you may be lucky enough to find the decision-maker, influencer and user are all the same person.

But you may also find yourself in a situation where different people have different buying roles. If the purchase affects a number of departments it can be even more complicated. For instance, the purchase of a new marketing automation system may require input from the finance, IT, marketing, product, ordering and fulfillment departments.

This is why the B2B buying process can be such a complex and challenging beast to navigate.

To get buyers purchasing your company's products and services, you need an in-depth understanding of:

- the company's business, including its strategies, business model, financials, industry trends and dynamics (which you would have gained from listening to the market and the customer)
- any key business issues and challenges—problems the buyers want to address and resolve, or opportunities they want to pursue
- their priorities and objectives, such as:

  - Achieving strategic or financial goals at a company level
  - Achieving individual goals (e.g. promotions, bonuses, recognition from industry peers)

How business buyers 'buy'

Buyers, influencers and change agents gain insights to help them with their key business objectives and evaluate a potential product or service provider from:

- case studies
- testimonials
- content that helps them meet their goals (e.g. articles, e-books, videos, blogs, video blogs)
- customer references
- online searches
- referrals and recommendations from peers, colleagues and industry experts
- endorsements and recommendations from micro-influencers within their target industries and markets

Recent studies show that 84% of B2B buyers now start the purchasing process with a referral, and peer recommendations influence more than 90% of all B2B buying decisions[14].

As a rule of thumb, buyers and influencers in a company will often use three sources as part of their 'shopping experience'. You need to know which ones will have the most impact on the decision-makers, influencers and change agent/mobilizer.

You'll need to make those key sources a core component of your B2B customer plans, which we'll discuss later in the book.

How business buyers evaluate your offering

The specific criteria buyers and influencers use to evaluate your product or service offering include:

- **Specific performance statistics:** Business buyers may want to see evidence of the benefits your company's offering and/or services will provide. The performance metrics buyers may use to evaluate them include:

- return on investment
- increased productivity
- increased sales
- cost savings
- increased revenue for the customer.

- **Meeting specific business outcomes and targets:** Your company may also be able to help business buyers set specific targets, which may be looked upon very favorably in the purchasing process. This involves knowing what their KPIs are and aligning them to your company's performance objectives.

- **Certifications and/or accreditations:** Some business buyers regard these as 'a ticket to the game' for considering a potential product or service provider. So as you research industries, markets or even potential customers, try to find out if there are any 'must-haves'. These requirements are often specified by:

  - corporate sourcing and procurement (e.g. ISO, project management certifications, etc.)
  - IT requirements (e.g. information security controls and data handling protocols, disaster recovery processes and resources etc.)

- **Expertise and/or specialization in specific industries and/or capabilities:** Don't let your company fall victim to 'marketing myopia'—defining your offer too narrowly. You'll end up focusing on areas of specialization and expertise in the hopes of marketing and selling more of your company's offerings without 'listening' (i.e. understanding) and responding to changing market and customer needs at a more general level.

  The best way to demonstrate expertise is through case studies, customer references, and having client-facing staff with significant industry experience.

- **Product features and functionalities:** You need to keep these simple, and anchor them to benefits for the customer and decision-makers. A list of features and functionalities can quickly become a complex and meaningless list of words or terms that mean very little to whoever is making the decision, even though they mean a lot to the users.

Think about your product features and functionality, and determine which ones are key value-drivers and which ones are lower-level features. In other words, what's your 'killer app'?

- **Service level guarantees:** These guarantee that your company will perform activities (such as deliveries, responses to queries, fault restorations) within specific time frames.

  You need to know specifically what your customer wants. Do they want 24-7 support, 99.9% uptime, or deliveries within the hour? You need to get this right, and avoid guaranteeing things that don't matter. Remember these two acronyms:

  - **SMART**—Specific, Measurable, Achievable, Realistic, Timely.
  - **KISS**—Keep it Simple Stupid.

- **Long-term and/or on-site support:** If you're a consulting company, having staff on site is a huge opportunity. It can be a major drawcard to a big client. You can deliver a higher level of support, and make your client feel confident the job is getting done. Your on-site staff can also listen to what's going on every day, and capture learnings and client insights that will elude your competitors.

- **Reporting and training:** Provide additional products and/or services to deliver greater value. You could offer them training days, or deliver a monthly newsletter with industry news and updates on the latest features for customers.

  Reporting performance statistics against KPIs is vital. It reminds your customers that you're delivering to requirements and are a high-performance vendor.

- **Use of specific methodologies and/or processes:** In some industries (e.g. engineering, consulting and technology), methodologies such as ISO and Lean can also be regarded as 'a ticket to the game'. However, you need to demonstrate how using these approaches will create the desired outcomes for the company.

- **Access to industry leaders/experts:** Many senior-level buyers value vendors who can connect them with industry leaders and experts—'movers and shakers' and disruptors. They want to develop their professional networks and connect with people who can help them take their business to the next level.

Every time you introduce someone in this way, you're making a deposit into the bank of goodwill, and building connections between you and the senior decision-makers. You're also establishing your reputation as someone with a powerful network who supports the objectives of your client and their organization.

How to 'listen' to B2B customers

We've found four listening methods that are very effective in getting an in-depth understanding of B2B customers. Some listening methods are more strategic, allowing you to gain an insight into the buyers' broader strategic and financial priorities, motivations and requirements.

Other listening methods are more operational, and help provide insights into the product and service offerings themselves in terms of:

- specifications
- capabilities
- how they're used
- how they're supported.

Both methods are effective, as they allow your company to get close to your business customers and obtain the deep and specific insights you need to respond to their motivations, priorities and needs.

Strategic listening methods	Operational methods
Executive interviews	Strategic customer reviews
Customer advisory panels	
Decision maker summits	

Let's look at each approach:

Approach 1 – Executive interviews

These are in-depth (usually face-to-face) discussions with the executives of your current or prospective customers. It's an effective way to get a detailed understanding of their key priorities, challenges, motivations and requirements.

In face-to-face interviews you can capture the executive's full attention. You can also read and respond to non-verbal cues such as body language and facial expressions, which can reveal their perspective on a particular issue.

Approach 2 – Customer advisory panels (CAPs)

The customer advisory panel (also known as the client advisory council) is a program that's often used to drive B2B sales and marketing. It involves regularly meeting with a small group of influential customers who have a vested interest in shaping your company's strategy.

When conducted effectively, CAPs can be powerful listening tools. They can help your company identify growth opportunities, as well as product and service offerings, and will help you:

- establish (or maintain) long-term profitable relationships with panel members
- acquire the larger, more attractive target customers you seek.

Here are the main components and characteristics of CAPs.

CAP component or characteristic	Description
Participants	Buyer (senior-level participants) from selected customers to get their perspective from a higher/strategic level. (Ideally, they'll be highly influential and well-regarded amongst their peers in their industry)
Number of customers	Ideally 10 to 15 customers that represent a cross-section of the customer base
Frequency	Twice a year
Format	Face-to-face meeting (two-way dialogue)
Panel participant input	**Industry direction and trends** (e.g. state of industry, anticipated changes and impact) **Customer business challenges** (e.g. priorities, objectives, needs, how companies may change resource allocation in response to industry changes) **Customer functional challenges** Priorities, needs, challenges from both a functional and senior-management perspective
Host company input	Information shared may include: • upcoming priorities/direction • key initiatives • company competencies • ability to respond to customer needs • proposed business and service models • why customers buy from them

The benefits of customer advisory panels

CAPs can provide multiple benefits to your company in its growth pursuits, including:

- input and feedback on new offerings, service models or innovation initiatives
- early warnings of shifts in customer needs and emerging opportunities
- advice on approaching and appealing to similar prospects/target customers
- developing new revenue streams
- developing new customer advocates
- reducing customer churn

TIP

To ensure your company is getting the most relevant and 'fresh' perspectives, you should change the members of your customer panel every two years.

For more information on customer advisory panels, visit: **www.customeradvisoryboard.org**.

Approach 3 – Decision-maker summits

Decision-maker summits (also known as roundtables or forums) are invitation-only events hosted by a B2B company to discuss issues, challenges and aspirations important to decision-makers within customers, prospects and target accounts. Designed around peer-to-peer interaction, they allow the host, customers and prospects to learn about each other and come up with ideas that can translate into growth opportunities. It also gives the host company's best customers an opportunity to share their experiences working with the company.

Decision-maker summits can be large or small, and typically include keynote speakers, panel discussions and/or breakout sessions.

You don't have to be a large company to host a B2B decision-maker summit. They can be run on a very lean budget.

Benefits of decision-maker summits

Decision-maker summits provide benefits to both you as the host company and your customers and prospects.

Here are the key benefits.

Host company	Customers	Prospects
Accelerate sales process	Professional networking	Professional networking
Increase close rates	Thought leadership opportunity	Access to host executives
Gain industry knowledge	Access to host executives	Increased confidence in host company
Identify innovation and growth opportunities	Validation of supplier	Peer exchange - best practices - lessons learned
Build relationships	Peer exchange - best practices - lessons learned - new ideas	

Source: The B2B Executive Playbook by Sean Geehan, 2011

A study by the Geehan Group found that B2B companies that conducted one or more summits reported the following results:

	Increased spend	Sales cycle reduction	Close rates with attendees
Current customers	Up by 10-30%	Down by 10-30%	Up by 10-50%
Prospects		Down by 15-60%	Up by 30-300%

Source: The B2B Executive Playbook by Sean Geehan, 2011

Approach 4 – Strategic customer workshops/customer visits

These workshops involve cross-functional representation from both the B2B supplier and the customer or prospects. The aim is to have in-depth discussions about the product and service offerings and what's needed in terms of enhancements, modifications, support and service requirements.

If possible, you should also include buyers, influencers and change agents in these sessions to ensure buyer requirements are also being met.

We recommend conducting strategic customer workshops in person at least twice per year as either a half- or full-day workshop. If you can, conduct them at your customer's premises so you and your team can 'be in your client's world' and get a sense of their organization and how they operate.

The participants should be a mix of staff and senior management from key functions and departments such as operations, product development, marketing and IT. Having a cross-functional mix of participants:

- gives attendees the chance to 'get into the detail' and discuss planning, execution and operational considerations of the issues or initiatives being addressed
- gives your attending staff and management a deep understanding of your customer's needs, objectives and challenges
- allows your functional and technical experts to hear from clients directly, and see them operate in their own environment.

Chapter summary

You must identify and understand key stakeholders in the B2B buying process in terms of their:

- priorities
- requirements
- motivations
- preferences
- behaviors.

You can do it by using the listening techniques we discussed in this chapter.

But remember: listening to both the market and customers isn't a 'one-off' project. Just as your priorities and objectives will change, so too will those of your customers and prospects—quickly and continually. So you must listen to your customers and prospects regularly to keep up with new trends, as well as changes in buyer behavior, priorities and requirements.

By establishing a process to listen to the market and customers regularly, your company will be well positioned to identify and seize new opportunities. These will help your business not only grow but also defend itself against new markets, disruptors and competitive threats.

Take action now

Make a list of your top 3–5 current business customers (or your most sought-after prospects if you don't have any business customers yet).

1. What do you want to achieve with them?
2. For each customer/prospect:
   a. Who is the true buyer (decision maker) for your offering?
   b. Who are the buyer's inner circle members (i.e. likely influencers)?
   c. Who is a potential change agent?
3. What do you know about the buyers' motivations and 'silver bullets' that would make them want to buy from your company?
4. What insights could your company give that would provide value to the buyers, influencers and change agents of the customers/ prospects you're pursuing?

If you can't identify these key players, perhaps other people you know could help you, such as:

- your business contacts (or their contacts)
- other people within these target companies.

PART 2

INNOVATE to know how to win

Section overview

Now that you know how to 'listen' to get an understanding of your company, your markets and your customers, it's time to use that understanding to identify and implement innovations to drive the growth of your company.

We'll start by discussing how to identify opportunities from listening to 'you', the market and customers. Then we'll explain what we mean by 'innovation', why it's important, and the types of innovations you can adopt in your company.

Towards the end of this section we'll show you how to make innovation a core component of your company's strategy. And we'll explain how you can plan, execute and manage your innovation initiatives to maintain customer-driven growth.

CHAPTER 4

Identifying opportunities to innovate from listening

Chapter overview

In the first three chapters we outlined how to listen to:

- yourself and your company
- the market
- your customers.

And for each listening method, we identified ways to collect feedback and information.

Now it's time to discuss how you can use that feedback and information to identify innovation opportunities.

How to identify innovation opportunities by listening to customers

When listening to customers, be on the lookout for insights and opportunities via:

Customer frustrations and complaints

Your business customers, whether they're decision-makers or users, may be frustrated or have issues with your products, services and/or processes. It may be that the capabilities you promised aren't being delivered at the speed, quality or service levels they need. Or perhaps the associated support services and processes don't match your customer's preferences, or are difficult to use.

They may like the product, but the support process or invoicing process isn't at the same level.

In B2B, being easy to deal with is often a key requirement. So, when a customer expresses frustration with your product, service or support, use that opportunity to learn from their feedback and improve.

Extreme customers

If you can, put a system in place where you can get feedback from customers who:

- love you
- hate you
- have left
- never buy from you.

These 'extreme' customers can be particularly demanding and frustrating. But from a learning perspective, they're your most valuable customers.

Once you identify your extreme customers, it's worth approaching and engaging them with the right listening tool. You may discover new offerings or support options that could lead to new product and/or service innovations with much broader applicability to the market. You'll also be able to better manage their expectations, which tend to be higher than most customers.

Customer immersion

Using the strategic customer workshop/customer visits approach, spend a day at a customer's premises to 'live in their world' and learn about it. Observe their operations, and talk to their customer-facing and operational staff. Think about what you'd do in their shoes.

As a provider, look at your company from their perspective. Look for opportunities to change or improve not just what you deliver (i.e.

your products and/or services) but also *how* you deliver (i.e. processes, organizational or marketing functions). Consider developing customer maps that model how your customer operates. They can help you visually identify opportunities to improve and add value through innovation.

How to identify innovation opportunities by listening to your market

Innovation opportunities can stem from 'market listening' in areas such as:

Analogies

When you conduct your market analysis, look at what the best companies are doing, both in your own industry and others. Try to determine:

- what kinds of innovation drive their success
- whether those same innovations are applicable to your industry
- what you could do in the same way to create a market opportunity.

For example, ride sharing is part of the sharing economy. Could your company rent or lease its assets to other companies?

Trends

Innovation often results from trends that are 'surging' (i.e. have strong momentum in the market). A trend typically indicates a change in how a product or service is being delivered, creating an industry-wide shift in preferences that buyers quickly embrace. Trends can also be the result of businesses and/or end consumers changing their behavior or motivations.

By identifying industry trends early, you can ensure you're on the winning side of change. For example, two recent trends are:

1. People increasingly wanting to work for themselves as independent contractors or 'solopreneurs'

2. Larger businesses needing specialists and wanting to reduce consulting costs.

These trends have created a need for online talent platforms such as Expert 360 and Talmix who connect businesses with contract workers.

Competition

You can often find opportunities to innovate by examining what your competitors are offering. The aim here is to find gaps in their offerings ('white spaces') that you can fill with a new solution. You may also be able to expand or improve on their offerings.

Are there markets or customer segments with a sizeable demand that are under-served? You may be able to gain a competitive advantage by providing the same offering while improving on the products or service offered, or increasing the service levels and support.

At the very least, reviewing competitor offers lets you see where they have a superior offer to you, and helps you determine whether you need to change or innovate to stay relevant in the market.

Changes in attitudes

Changes in attitudes and views can create new opportunities. For instance, the global attitude towards startups has changed dramatically over the past ten years. A decade ago, startups were typically shunned by large companies, such as banks and other lending institutions, because they were considered 'unstable' and 'risky'. While startups still carry a high level of risk, they're now regarded as nimble, agile and effective at developing new concepts.

This has resulted in an array of products and services aimed at startups, including:

- collaboration software that allows them to work with large organizations on projects
- collaboration hubs that let startups/SMEs and large businesses co-locate and work together

- coaching services to teach startups and SMEs how to work together effectively, and then support them.

New technology and knowledge

New technology can provide opportunities for service innovation. The increasing use of virtual reality and artificial intelligence has created opportunities to provide consulting, coaching and training to end users and other affected business departments such as marketing, product development, contact centers and customer service.

How to identify innovation opportunities by listening to 'you'

Two more great sources of innovation opportunities are your company and you, as its owner/manager. You should examine yourself and your company closely to identify:

- key skills, talent and knowledge
- where you have a proven track record
- reviews of new product/service offerings or variations that were successful, as well as those that weren't so successful.

Once you've identified these internal knowledge resources, ask yourself and your team:

- Does the company have any skill, talent or knowledge that's being ignored or underutilized?
- What were the key factors of our successes and failures?
- Could we expand or improve any areas by using one or more types of innovation?
- Could those innovations be applied to other markets, customer segments or key accounts?

You can also tap into the power of you and your company by holding brainstorming sessions or innovation workshops. Bring your employees, suppliers, customers and partners together and see how you can make the most of your existing knowledge and expertise.

Chapter summary

Whether you're listening to 'you', the market or your customers, there are specific topics and issues you need to look for. They can serve as a beacon and highlight ways to implement various types of innovations.

Take action now

- Speak with your customer/client-facing staff such as your customer service reps or account managers and ask them:
  - about any key frustrations or issues they have with your company's products, services, support or processes
  - whether they experience any recurring issues or frustrations.
- Create ways to get feedback from your 'extreme' customers— those who love your company and those who hate it.
- If you haven't already done so, set up a strategic customer workshop or customer visit program for your company. Develop a schedule for your management team and people from across the business to spend a half or full day with some of your key customers. It will give them a deeper understanding of the business, and the priorities and concerns of the buyers and influencers within those organizations.
- Review the analysis and insights you obtained from listening to the market. Meet with members of your management team and ask:

- Are there gaps in competitive offers that we could fill?
- Are there deficiencies in competitive products that we could exploit and position around?
- Are there markets and/or customer segments whose needs aren't being met that could be an attractive growth opportunity?

- Identify key upcoming conferences, presentations and seminars that could give you insights into market trends, customer needs and perceptions, new technologies, or other developments. Have representatives from your company attend to capture key insights and report their findings to you and your management team.

CHAPTER 5

Defining innovation

Chapter overview

In this chapter we introduce the notion of 'business innovation' and the types of innovation you can implement in your business. We'll also discuss:

- the current levels of innovation among SMEs
- why innovation is so important
- the impact it can have on business performance.

This chapter will give you a better understanding of innovation, which will allow you to consider how the various types could be applied to your company and drive growth in your business.

We'll also discuss how to incorporate the identified innovation opportunities into your business strategy.

What is innovation?

If you asked our fellow startup and SME tribe members what they think innovation is, they'd probably tell you it's creating new products or leveraging new technology (often digitally based) to conduct business. But while these are both good examples, innovation is more than just creating another digital business plan platform or sexy new product that customers line up days in advance for.

Innovation can be defined as **introducing something new or making a significant improvement** in one or more of these areas:

- Products and services – the offerings delivered to customers
- Organizational methods – the structure of the business
- Marketing practices – how the business positions and promotes itself
- Business processes – processes that reduce costs or improve efficiency and/or effectiveness in servicing customers[15].

Innovation that's viewed in this broader context is called **business innovation.**

Business innovation is more about creating new types of *value* than creating new things. It goes beyond *what* you produce to *how* you produce and market it. It's a more strategic mindset that sees your business as an integrated system where innovation can be applied at all levels—from sourcing to production to delivery. Of course, it should also be applied to the product or service itself.

You must think of innovation as more than just new products or technologies, and consider it from the broader context of **business innovation.** As innovation expert Mohan Sawnhey points out, viewing innovation too narrowly "blinds companies to opportunities and leaves them vulnerable to competitors with broader perspectives"[16].

If you don't adopt this broader view of innovation, your competitors will pursue the same customers with similar offerings and innovate in the same ways with the same undifferentiated capabilities. For instance, in technology industries, most firms focus on product innovation[17]. This has led to the commoditization of many product and service offerings, making it difficult for startups to differentiate and compete.

A cursory review of the Android or iOS app store shows this clearly, and the outcome has been increased price competition. The challenges of achieving growth across different industries and international markets makes it crucial for business innovation to become a core component of your company's strategy.

Business innovation can occur at three levels:

- **New to the world:** These are groundbreaking, and what most people think of as innovation. But groundbreaking innovations are comparatively rare. And when they do occur, they can't always be commercialized.
- **New to the market or industry:** This involves taking a concept or idea from one industry, and applying it to another industry in a new way, context or situation.
- **New to the company:** This type of innovation is about creating the latest products and services by applying organizational methods, marketing practices or business processes to compete more effectively[18].

Two pathways to business innovation

Your startup or SME can adopt two approaches to drive business innovation:

1. Disruptive or radical innovation
2. Incremental innovation

1. Disruptive or radical innovation

Radical innovations improve products or services in ways the markets or industries don't expect. They may redefine the way customers do things, or deliver value that customers haven't thought of themselves. This often leads to 'new to the world' or 'new to market or industry' innovations.

Disruptive innovations can be very risky because they:

- require a substantial investment of money, time and resources
- often have a high degree of uncertainty.

They may also involve significant technological changes, or the invention of new ones.

Business model innovation (BMI)

One type of radical innovation established SMEs in particular may wish to consider is business model innovation. A business model is the set of decisions that defines how your SME keeps going and makes money. These decisions form the backbone of the company and include:

- Mission, vision and core values
- core resources
- target markets and customers
- customer offerings
- customer experience
- channel strategy.

BMI can disrupt current business and operations, which can be risky. It's both highly challenging and disruptive, as the change will focus on the strategies, processes and capabilities that made the company successful. But for some established SMEs, the transformation can be the key to its long-term survival, especially in situations where they face irrelevance or obsolescence[19].

Indicators for business model change include:

- declining industry margins
- being unable to keep up with changes in the industry
- the opportunity to use current product/service offerings to serve customers in outside industries.

2. Incremental innovation

These are small improvements over time that can have a significant impact on both your company's financials and the value given to customers.

In a B2B context they can be driven by:

- market, industry or business customer needs
- requirements or feedback from suppliers, partners and end customers.

Incremental innovations can involve enhancements or improvements to existing products, services and processes. They're often less risky, and don't require large capital investment or assets compared to business model innovation. Instead, they apply current core competencies and capabilities, with perhaps some modest enhancements or a slight shift in method.

This makes incremental innovation far more realistic and feasible for most startups and SMEs.

Consider how your company allocates its resources across the two innovation pathways. While you may wish to allocate some resources towards larger, riskier innovation initiatives, incremental innovations should be at the core of your company's innovation strategy.

This concept naturally lends itself to the Growth Horizons model, where different levels of focus and resources are invested according to risk and return relative to current business models.

Factors that determine the attractiveness and feasibility of an incremental innovation include:

- the impact on customers (especially your strategic customers)
- the investment required
- the time to market
- the amount of change required in terms of:
  - processes
  - systems/platforms
  - staff
- the impact on your products, services, and ability to support and service your business customers.

Depending on the type of incremental innovation you're undertaking, you can apply a variety of approaches and tactics such as:

- design thinking
- process mapping
- customer experience journey mapping
- ideation (brainstorming) sessions.

While such methodologies are beyond the scope of this book, there are plenty of books and other resources on these topics if you need more information on these approaches.

The key to determining how to innovate is knowing how much value it will give your customers. In terms of business customers this means knowing:

- what you deliver—your products and services (product/service innovation)
- how you deliver—your processes and organizational methods (process/organizational innovation)
- how you promote—your marketing practices (marketing innovation).

All three areas must meet and respond to your business customers' needs.

Why is innovation important?

Innovating in more than one area can lead to greater earnings. Studies have shown that:

- innovating in one area resulted in an average improvement of $386,000.
- innovating in two areas resulted in an average improvement of $392,000.
- innovating in 3–4 areas resulted in an average improvement of $763,000[20].

Maintaining or growing current revenue is a key concern for many SMEs in Australia, including those in industries such as:

- information, media and telecommunications
- professional, scientific and technical services
- financial and insurance services[21].

Unfortunately, despite this fact:

- 56% of Australian businesses don't innovate[22]
- 52% of Canadian businesses with less than 100 staff don't innovate
- 42% of Canadian businesses with between 100 and 499 staff don't innovate[23].

Businesses that *do* innovate will probably implement only one type of innovation. Process innovation is the most common type of innovation utilized due to the new technology that's becoming available. Many SMEs use technology to:

- replace manual processes
- move infrastructure to the cloud
- implement new IT systems.

Taking on multiple forms of business innovation isn't easy. But plenty of startups and SMEs have looked at their business customers' needs and value requirements and innovated successfully, with resultant growth in B2B markets.

One example is Silfab Solar, an SME based in Mississauga, Canada. Silfab makes solar modules for commercial use, and has grown by undertaking the following business innovations:

- **Marketing innovation:** Silfab has expanded from operating solely in Canada to operating in global markets such as the United States and Mexico. Exports now account for almost 90% of the company's revenue[24].
- **Process innovation—co-creation:** Silfab partnered with solar photo voltaic (PV) technology company Morgan Solar to design, develop and mass-produce low-cost PV modules specifically for large commercial and utility scale projects[25].

Chapter summary

Innovation goes beyond developing new products and technologies. You can use four types of business innovation to significantly grow your business.

By going beyond product and service innovation, your company can differentiate itself to not only compete but also drive growth.

But the key to innovating successfully is making sure that every innovation delivers value to both your customers and your business.

In the next chapter, we'll go into detail about how to apply these four types of innovations in a B2B context.

Take action now

Meet with your leadership team and do the following:

- Consider your key customers and prospects and ask yourselves:

  - What do these customers value from a B2B supplier? Remember to think in terms of buyers (decisions makers, internal influencers and change agents) and end users, as they may define value from a supplier differently.

  - Can we address any of these requirements with the four types of business innovations?

- Review your company's operations in the context of the four types of business innovations.

- Which ones are you currently doing?

- Are there opportunities to expand your business innovation endeavors?

CHAPTER 6

Where to apply B2B innovation

Chapter overview

In this chapter you'll learn how to apply business innovation in a B2B context. We'll talk about the types of business innovation you can use to meet the needs of your business customers and drive business growth. We'll also discuss the characteristics and key components of each type of innovation, as well as key considerations and potential next steps.

By the end of the chapter you'll be able to discuss them with your management team and decide which innovation approaches to apply to your business.

Business innovation in your business

Remember, your company's innovation efforts should be driven by:

1. **Listening to the market** to make sure they're based on your customers' and prospects' needs, and the outcomes and value they want—not what they explicitly ask for.

2. **Listening to 'you'** to make sure they're based on your understanding of the core skills, assets and capabilities your company has (or can acquire).

Failure to do so will result in your startup or SME:

- trying to satisfy all customers, which can lead to dissatisfaction
- focusing on projects and initiatives that aren't aligned with your core business, strengths and capabilities.

Five key principles to guide your company's B2B innovation efforts

To ensure you have a planned and strategic approach to your company's innovation endeavors, here are five key principles your company should understand and refer back to:

1. **The Pareto principle:** In most businesses, 20% of your customers will account for 80% of your revenue. You need to look after them.

2. **The true customer knowledge principle:** You need to develop a deep understanding of what customers want and value—even when they may not understand themselves.

3. **The multi-tenanting principle:** You should never build a process or innovation more than once if you can build it once and copy it.

4. **The problem-solving principle:** It's okay to promise you'll deliver more tomorrow than you can deliver today if you have the ingenuity and resources to bridge the gap.

5. **The expectation management principle:** There's no point in over-promising if you can't deliver. Know and state your true limitations.

With these principles in mind, remember that true business innovation means innovating in one or more areas. Here's an overview of the five innovation areas, and the types of business innovation approaches you can use for each.

Innovation area	True innovation
Product	New product lines New products Product extensions Product redesign Product enhancements
Services	New service offerings Service redesign Service enhancements
Organizational	Outsourcing Strategic alliances Restructures New training program implementations
Marketing	Entering new markets New distribution/sales channels New marketing strategies and approaches such as pricing strategies
Process	New operational processes New customer service/buying processes New processes to understand customer needs (customer insight)

Source: CommBank Business Insights Report by Commonwealth Bank of Australia, 2017

To drive growth in your company, you should ideally be driving innovation in at least two areas.

Let's discuss the five innovation areas in detail, and how they can be used in a B2B context.

Product innovation

Before we start discussing product innovation in a B2B context, let's quickly define what we mean by a product.

A product is an item of value that satisfies a demand. It can be tangible (e.g. in a physical form such as a computer or plant and equipment) or intangible (e.g. insurance, or cloud storage), and the customer takes possession by purchasing or renting it.

Product innovation can include:

- launching new products
- extending existing product lines
- transforming existing offerings through extensive redesign.

To drive growth in their companies, startups and SMEs must focus on true product innovation (i.e. 'new to the market' or 'new to their industry' innovation). To develop new product innovations, your company must:

- use product development approaches specifically suited to B2B
- always consider the needs of business customers as a motivating force.

(Please note: product development is a significant discipline in its own right, and beyond the scope of this book. There are numerous resources available online that go into the detail of product design.)

In B2B there are two key ways to engage customers in product development:

1. Many startups and SMEs use the Lean Startup methodology. This methodology is based on a **'Build-Measure-Learn'** process whereby a prototype is created (Build), tested with customers (Measure) and then changed based on the feedback obtained (Learn).
2. While this approach is fine in a Business-to-Consumer (B2C) context, the cost of prototyping in B2B can be quite high, with

lengthy timelines involved. So instead you should incorporate a **Learn-Build-Measure-Learn** process, where you engage with customers before you even develop a hypothesis, let alone a prototype.

Here's why it's important to engage with business customers early in the product development process.

- B2B companies are generally driven by economic and financial decisions and objectives. These decisions can be discussed and predicted before customers experience the product or service.
- B2B customers are knowledgeable and technically adept. They can provide valuable input about their business and industry, which will help in the development process.
- The highly concentrated nature of B2B markets (i.e. where ten customer accounts can constitute 50% or more of the total market buying power) means understanding a small number of customers can give you a deep understanding of **market** needs[26].

Example of customer engagement in product development

Ikabo is a startup technology company based in Sydney, Australia with a core product based on SAAS technology. The Ikabo Incubator leverages an online crowdsourcing platform to provide services related to:

- customer and employee engagement
- innovation and strategic thinking.

Customer engagement has been an integral part of Ikabo's product development.

INITIAL PROTOTYPE/ MINIMUM VIABLE PRODUCT (MVP)

The Ikabo Incubator was first developed after conducting 30 in-depth interviews with potential customers to understand their needs, challenges and problems.

ONGOING PRODUCT DEVELOPMENT

Maintaining an in-depth understanding of business customer needs is a core component of Ikabo's ongoing product development. The Ikabo team regularly conducts strategic customer selling meetings to understand customer requirements, challenges and issues.

At the end of every client engagement they conduct a review (the 'Customer Retrospective') to understand what they learned, key success factors, and areas for improvement.

They conduct their debriefs with the product development team to give them feedback, which is also captured in Ikabo's Market Requirements Document. This 'living' document contains all market, competitor and customer information, and is regularly updated, reviewed and discussed at the quarterly product development meetings.

To learn more about Ikabo and its journey to *Listen, Innovate and Grow*, check out the case study chapter at the end of the book.

Service innovation

Before we talk about service innovation in a B2B context, let's define what we mean by a service.

A service is an activity or function that is purchased once and has a finite life. Once a service is consumed, used or delivered, it must be replaced.

The customer often participates in providing or consuming the service. For instance, you have to get on the plane and fly to the destination for that important business meeting to have used the airline's services. You have to attend meetings and presentations or read reports to consume accounting, consulting or legal services.

As a result of this participatory characteristic, services provide significant opportunities to be more innovative and interactive.

Benefits of B2B-focused service innovation

Undertaking service innovations that focus on business customers can benefit your company by:

- creating new services and products you can sell to current and prospective customers and create incremental revenue opportunities
- closely integrating you with your customers, creating stronger barriers to exit that allow you to charge a premium for your services
- creating deeper customer relationships that have more diverse revenue streams.

Three ways to innovate your service offering

Startups and SMEs looking to undertake service innovation within a B2B context should consider these three approaches:

1. Digitize your offerings

Determine whether there are opportunities to convert manual processes, physical products or traditional services into mobile or web-based offerings—even those you take for granted. For instance, letting your business customers collect and interpret data through their mobile devices will give them fast and convenient access to knowledge and information.

2. Expand according to your strengths

Consider creating new services that:

- compliment what your company is already successfully doing
- address additional customer needs you've identified by 'listening' to them.

Areas that you can expand your services include training, workshops, consulting, reporting and analytics.

Example of using existing capability to expand services

Empower Construction, based in Sydney, Australia, provides external cladding to residential and commercial builders. (Cladding provides a degree of thermal insulation and water resistance to a building, and improves its appearance.)

Empower's founder Ryan Steyn conducts face-to-face meetings with key decision makers (i.e. the national and regional construction managers within his clients) every six months.

By listening to the feedback, Ryan and his team saw an opportunity to solve a problem clients were experiencing, and deliver more value. Empower expanded its offering to include rendering and painting, thereby allowing Empower to significantly increase its revenue by providing more services.

To learn more about Empower and its journey to *Listen, Innovate and Grow*, check out their case study at the end of the book.

3. Meet the bigger customer need

Become the 'one stop shop' for your customers by creating comprehensive customer solutions—bundles of products, services, support and information that help them achieve a specific objective or outcome.

COMPONENTS OF A CUSTOMER SOLUTION

As well as your company's main product or service offering, a business customer solution or package can consist of:

- additional services such as:
  - training
  - delivery
  - consulting/advice
  - reporting
  - industry/market research
  - maintenance
  - problem solving
  - outsourcing (i.e. performing tasks that customer does not wish to perform)
- customer support provisions such as:
  - extended hours of operation
  - choice of service delivery channels (e.g. face-to-face, phone)
  - service level guarantees (e.g. query or maintenance response times)
  - financing (e.g. payment and warranty options).

While you can design and offer customer solutions to practically any business customer, they're particularly common in industries such as:

- IT
- telecommunications
- financial services
- professional services (e.g. accounting, consulting, law, marketing).

Some examples of customer bundles or packages are:

- a marketing consulting firm offering a business marketing package to companies that includes:

- the marketing strategy
- sales tools and marketing collateral
- website development
- specified number of hours of marketing campaign support
- an IT company offering prepaid support packages that include:
  - help desk/onsite support
  - project planning and management
  - backup monitoring
  - server maintenance and administration.

Providing business customer packages can be a big win for your company. And your business customers will benefit from customized solutions that meet specific objectives and outcomes.

Organizational innovation

Organizational innovation is about implementing a new organizational method in the firm's business practices, workplace organization and external relations[27] such as:

- strategic alliances
- partnerships
- outsourcing business functions
- organizational restructures.

It can be a challenging area for startups and SMEs that are busy with the day-to-day of 'working in the business'. (It's the type of innovation least pursued by SMEs[28].)

But given the increased competitiveness and rapid change brought on by new technologies, increasing digitization and changing trends, startups and SMEs need to develop new business models, strategies and approaches to remain relevant. And organizational innovation can help them compete and grow in today's challenging and rapidly changing environment.

One form of organizational innovation startups and SMEs should consider is collaborating with other startups and SMEs, as well as larger organizations such as universities and corporates. Startups and SMEs can use collaboration to access and leverage new ideas, skills, technologies and equipment. It can help them develop new products and services, and drive other forms of business innovation. Third parties can also give them access to influencers and new customers, which are both fundamental to driving growth.

Collaborating with larger organizations can unlock the resources and expertise you need to quickly scale up your business significantly.

Large corporates are increasingly open to working with startups and SMEs. They value their agility, and their ability to develop successful concepts and value propositions without being encumbered by large monolithic organizational structures.

You can identify opportunities for collaboration in your business by:

- conducting research to identify companies with the knowledge, skills, resources, customers and contacts that can complement your business
- identifying innovation or collaboration hubs that can link your company with other organizations that may give you the resources and capabilities you lack
- identifying relevant consortia in your industry that help startups and SMEs grow by promoting collaboration and knowledge transfer between universities, corporates and SMEs.

Examples of collaboration with SMEs

CRIBIQ, a Quebec City-based consortium that promotes collaborative research project in bioprocessed and bio sourced products, fostered a relationship between:

- Atrium Innovation, a large natural health product company
- Nutra Canada, an SME specializing in fruit, vegetable and medicinal extracts.

The two companies are working together to develop and commercialize new cranberry extracts that can be used to create innovative consumers products[29].

Process innovation

Process innovation is about introducing new production or delivery methods to help a company compete, meet customer needs and/or improve efficiency.

As you can imagine, it can be done in any number of ways. But we want to focus on a particular method for creating products and services in B2B: co-creating them with your customers. Or as we like to call it, B2B Customer Innovation (B2B-CI).

B2B-CI consists of working with a handful of customers with long-term strategic value to co-create and innovate. So rather than choosing customers at random, you're looking for:

- the top 5-20% customers in terms of revenue or margins
- customers who can help you achieve other key strategic objectives, such as penetrating new markets or industries.

With B2B-CI, you focus on uncovering specific issues and opportunities that can deliver significant value to the individual customer[30]. The aim is to create **mutual value** for both your company and the individual customers you collaborate with.

B2B-CI should allow your company to make the solution set more applicable, as the solutions you develop will be applicable to other segments, markets and industries. This is often referred to as the **multi-tenanting** principle: a solution or product for one group can be cost-effectively scaled to many customers, driving revenue higher than the marginal cost of delivery.

B2B-CI will provide a number of benefits to your company, including:

- increased spend with existing customers through upsell and cross-sell opportunities
- increased supplier exclusivity (i.e. your company is the sole provider)
- greater customer credibility, access and retention
- ideas that wouldn't have been thought of in other circumstances
- R&D with built-in testers, case studies and testimonials.

Key success factors for B2B-CI

The success of B2B-CI in your company will rely on your company having these factors in place:

- Focusing on your Top 20 customers (the Pareto principle).
- Support of your company's leadership and their advocacy of the B2B-CI approach, which you must communicate regularly throughout the company.
- People who confidently believe they have the resources and capabilities to leverage opportunities identified through B2B-CI. (The confidence and belief come from the support of your senior leadership team.)

- A leadership team that has a very strong understanding of your customers':

  - environment and organizational goals
  - key issues, objectives and challenges

- Sponsorship and endorsement by a non-sales decision-maker within your customer. (A non-sales focus is about genuinely creating value for the customer, not sales.)

This in-depth understanding and decision-maker endorsement will allow your company to engage the appropriate people and get them to work with the customer's team.

An example of B2B-CI in action

One of Evolve's key clients is Coles, a leading Australian supermarket chain. Since Evolve's inception we've focused on Coles' needs, and been attuned to meeting its business requirements in a myriad of ways.

In our initial engagement with Coles, it became clear that delivering customer feedback to store managers quickly was a key requirement, and would likely have broader applications.

Focusing on Coles' requirements for real-time online reporting of customer feedback, Evolve developed a range of online dashboard reporting technologies. Rather than receiving customer feedback each quarter, store managers can now log into an online reporting environment and absorb customer feedback from the previous week.

To develop this technology we needed considerable capital investment in our survey platform, data warehouse capability and online reporting tools. Our developers worked with the complete support of management, and were given significant technology resources to achieve the goal.

By learning from Coles' needs, we created a generic capability that many other clients have adopted to mutual benefit.

Marketing innovation

Marketing innovation is about implementing new marketing strategies and approaches that are significantly different to your company's existing methods.

Marketing innovations are aimed at:

- better addressing customer needs
- opening up or entering new markets
- positioning a company's products or services.

All of which are aimed at increasing sales from existing customers and acquiring new customers[31].

Marketing innovations commonly used by startups and SMEs

Marketing innovations that startups and SMEs typically use to drive growth include:

- specialization
- geographic expansion
- brand/line extension.

Let's take a look at each one.

Specialization

Specialization is a marketing strategy that startups and SME growth managers often explore to drive growth. It supports delivering a more narrowly defined offer that's superior to alternatives from competitors who have diluted their focus across a range of products and solutions.

Companies can specialize in one or more of the following:

- specific markets, customers
- customer segments

- industries
- products
- services.

Specialization is a key strategic component of many high-growth firms (i.e. firms that have maintained annual revenue growth of 20% or more over a three-year period)[32].

Geographic expansion

Geographic expansion is about offering your products and services to new markets—domestic and/or international. You have an opportunity to expand your market when:

- there's an identified market need for your offering
- you have limited competition, or you can differentiate your offering strongly
- the cost of market entry isn't prohibitive
- your company has enough knowledge about the market's dynamics, characteristics, customer requirements and buying behavior
- your company has an appropriate 'Go to Market' strategy, and the skills, capabilities and resources to execute it.

Your ability to grow through geographic expansion will depend on the type of business you operate. For example, location is largely irrelevant to a technology business selling software as a service (SAAS) predominantly online.

To enter new markets and sell your services there, you need to leverage marketing channels that:

- have the required reach
- are used by the business customers you're targeting.

However, a professional services business may find expanding into new markets challenging. There could be significant costs in terms of travel, time, offices and staff, not to mention the potential need for local market expertise. These costs and challenges need to be weighed up against the potential benefits of an increased client base, greater market coverage and overall profitability.

Your expansion plans can also be impeded by culture, language and regulations. A significant growth opportunity for your business could be undermined simply because you:

- can't communicate in the language
- don't understand the culture, regulations and ways of doing business in international markets.

To avoid these issues, get professional advice.

Many countries have public sector organizations that will provide you with:

- information on regulations and ways of doing business
- resources to help you establish your company locally.

Brand/line extension

Brand and line extensions can be great strategies for creating new revenue opportunities and growing your business.

A brand and line extension is where you expand your offers by creating:

- entirely new products and services
- new variations of existing product or service offerings.

The key is to think beyond what your business does and offers today. If you don't, the result will be **marketing myopia**—a concept first introduced by Theodore Levitt in 1960. Levitt said businesses that define what they do too narrowly risk market obsolescence. To grow, companies must recognize that customer needs change over time.

Why startups and SMEs must adopt new marketing innovations to win in B2B

It's important for companies pursuing B2B to move beyond traditional marketing approaches such as advertising and social media to promote their offerings. While such approaches may generate awareness, they aren't effective at getting business buyers to purchase.

A B2B marketing study conducted in 2017 showed that 79% of business buyers knew of at least three suppliers at the start of the buying process, and 28% didn't look for additional suppliers[33].

And the top three methods buyers used to look for potential suppliers at the start of the process were:

- internet search (39%)
- referrals from professional advisors (34%)
- talking to colleagues and peers (33%)

As a startup or SME pursuing growth through business markets, you must focus your B2B marketing on creating awareness and engagement among the buying group (i.e. buyers and internal influencers) of your customers and prospects before they start looking to buy.

You can do this by:

- providing advice and recommendations
- providing insights about the industry, markets and customers
- identifying opportunities that address their needs, priorities and strategic objectives, and help them build and grow their businesses.

Two marketing innovations startups and SMEs must adopt to drive growth

Every startup or SME that wants to grow through B2B markets must incorporate two marketing innovations as part of their B2B company strategy:

1. Advocacy marketing
2. Influencer marketing

As you'll soon learn, these low-cost methods are both highly effective at getting the customers and clients you want to grow your company.

1. Advocacy marketing

Advocacy marketing is about using existing clients and customers who are strong advocates of your company (i.e. your 'raving fans') to endorse and promote your products and services to other prospects. It's effective because customers find the peer-to-peer dialogue more trustworthy, authentic and relevant.

But to get the most out of these approaches they must be centralized, coordinated, and formalized into a B2B customer advocacy program.

Advocacy marketing is made up of referrals and references. Let's look at each one in more detail.

REFERRALS

Referrals are buyer endorsements from trusted people such as colleagues, employees and friends. Buyers generally want endorsement from people with a good knowledge of the product or service they want to buy. Despite the volume of generic advice and content available, buyers still rely heavily on their own network for referrals and references when making a decision.

Fact: A study of more than 600 B2B organizations in Canada and the United States found that 84% of B2B decision makers start the buying process with a referral[34].

Referrals can have a positive impact on B2B company performance. A study of companies with referral programs found that:

- 59% reported higher customer lifetime values
- 71% reported higher conversion rates

However, only 30% of B2B companies have a formalized referral program[35].

To keep getting maximum effectiveness from referrals, you must establish a formalized program so you know:

- what types of referrals to seek
- when to ask for a referral
- how to ask for a referral
- how to manage the referral both internally and with the referee.

The key to a successful referral program is to keep engaging with your customers by providing:

- value-added content and advice
- opportunities for your customers to interact with you and each other.

This will build a sense of delight among your customers and make them more willing to refer and create referral opportunities.

Tips to Establish a Formal Referral Program

1. Tell advocates what you're looking for in an ideal prospect

- Types of organizations
- Roles you want to connect with
- Business problems they may face

2. Make it easy to refer

- Identify the best (and preferred) ways for advocates to send referrals (e.g. phone, email, online referral page)
- Have tools and processes in place to make referrals easier to manage and distribute to your sales/client teams for follow-up.

3. Know when to ask for a referral

- Find points of delight along the customer journey when it would be an opportune time to ask for a referral.

4. Define how referrals will be managed

- Determine how the referees will be managed
- Determine how you'll follow up with the advocate that referred you

5. Provide rewards and recognition

- Determine how you'll reward and recognize your advocates. Rewards shouldn't just be monetary. Suitable options include:
    - Free product
    - Free service upgrade
    - Free report
    - First opportunity to trial a new offering
    - Opportunities for professional development
    - Exclusive access to a C-level event
    - A way for advocates to promote themselves and their companies through opportunities such as guest speaking at events, podcasts
    - Contests and promotions.[36]

Example of SME advocacy marketing success: The Ecobee company

Ecobee is an SME based in Toronto, Canada that produces Wi-Fi-enabled smart thermostats for residential and commercial applications. Founded in 2007, it currently has around 40 employees, and it has leveraged the power of advocates to drive the company's growth.

They established a community of advocates, the VIBees, which the company relies on heavily in its growth and innovation initiatives. For instance, Ecobee established an "Access Behind the Curtain" initiative where new products are launched with advocates first to get their feedback. Customer service and product processes are also established and adjusted with advocates as their focus.

Other advocacy initiatives include:

- **Feature Fridays:** Advocates write blogs about different elements of Ecobee products
- **Following the Conversation:** Ecobee engages in dialogue with its online community
- Advocates taking selfies and posting personal stories online about how smart thermostats have improved their lives
- Members of the Ecobee leadership team meeting with advocates while traveling.

Ecobee's strong focus on advocacy marketing has contributed to the company being the number two player in the smart thermostat market globally, competing with Fortune 500 companies such as Google and Honeywell[36].

REFERENCES

A reference is a customer who is willing to speak on your behalf to potential customers about:

- what products and services your company provided
- the effect it had on their business
- their experience of working with you.

As with referrals, references are a simple but effective marketing tactic to use in a B2B context. Business buyers are people, and people like to deal with other people they know, trust and will help make them successful.

A vital component of your marketing strategy is to use clients, customers and industry peers as advocates and champions, who then encourage others to buy your products and services.

An effective way of doing this is to establish a customer reference program (CRP). B2B companies set up these programs to gather and fulfill customer references to help companies obtain new clients. Decision-makers and influencers often look for these references when making high-value and high-risk purchases.

When they're implemented effectively, CRPs can:

- accelerate the sales process by 20-60%
- increase closing rates by from 30-150%[37]

Typical customer reference activities

Your CRP may involve activities such as:

- case studies/success stories
- video testimonials
- prospects visiting customer premises
- customers speaking on behalf of your company to media and/or at industry or company events.

The activities you use for your customers will be determined by:

- where your buyers look
- what they want to look at
- who they want to speak to.

Asking customers to participate in a CRP is like making a withdrawal or request based on the goodwill of your customers. You'll need to provide rewards and incentives to encourage them to participate. You'll also need to consider what rewards the members of the buying group in your participating companies will value. For example, you could offer:

- free product trials
- professional development
- invitations to special industry VIP events.

Key success factor for customer reference programs: buyer appeal

To maximize the benefit your company gets from your CRP, you must get executive references (i.e. references from your buyers' senior level peers). And not just those who appeal to users. Your ultimate objective is to get the buyers to buy, and so you need references that will appeal to them. Your references should demonstrate how your company helped them achieve some of their higher level and broader objectives as well as the user requirements.

Core activities in setting up and managing a customer reference program

Here are the four key steps to setting up and managing an effective CRP:

1. Recruit highly satisfied clients/customers.
2. Create reference materials (case studies, performance statistics, video testimonials, etc.) that demonstrate the customer's experience and your company's impact. Use the insights you get from your buyers inner circle and shopping experience to choose the most appropriate reference materials.
3. Manage reference requests. Depending on the number of requests you may choose to:

   - manage these through an internal site
   - have one of your team members manage the requests
   - outsource it to a marketing agency/service provider.

4. Measure the results to determine the effectiveness of the materials/ approaches and the number of deals closed.

For more information on CRPs refer to:

- Our website: listeninnovategrow.com
- The Customer Reference Handbook
- The Customer Reference Forum Association

Influencer marketing

Influencer marketing is where leaders and experts in your niche/industry promote and endorse your company and its offerings. It's another effective way to boost and promote your company authentically.

Why is influencer marketing important?

When B2B buyers are researching a purchase, they look for more than just product and service details. They want a real connection with the companies providing the products and services. Many B2B brands don't stand out because they don't establish that connection[38].

But when B2B buyers are *considering* a purchase, the sources they turn to after searching the web are peers, colleagues and industry experts. Carefully selected influencers can provide the relevancy, trust and authenticity buyers are looking for.

Two types of influencers for B2B startups and SMEs

Startups and SMEs should look for two types of influencers as part of their marketing strategy.

1. The independent influencer

This is someone who specializes in an area and has built an audience around their personal brand and expertise *without* any links to a specific company. They have a significant audience/following on social media (Twitter, LinkedIn, etc.)—at least 2,000, but usually tens of thousands, and they're willing to work with companies in their specialty area.

2. The micro-influencer

These people also focus on a specific area of knowledge. However, they tend to have a small to moderate following (less than 2,000 people). Given their smaller following, micro-influencers may be more willing to work with your startup or SME on mutually-beneficial endeavors.

Benefits of influencers

Influencers can help drive the growth of your startup or SME by :

- raising your company's profile
- providing access to a specific audience for a product or service launch
- helping you and your company establish expertise in a specialization
- helping your company establish its presence in a new industry or market.

For example, your startup or SME could use an influencer :

- to impartially review your product or service
- as a guest for your blog or podcast.

How to identify influencers

Identifying influencers isn't easy. It takes time and effort to identify appropriate people for both your company and the specific areas of specialization.

The best way to start is by searching online using relevant keywords. Once you've identified a list of potential influencers, research their thought leadership content (articles, blog posts, podcasts, etc.) to:

- understand their point of view and perspective on their area of expertise
- get to know them in terms of their personality and how they want to engage.

This is important, as the next step is to contact them.

Building a relationship with influencers takes time and effort. While you'll probably contact them online, you may also need some face-to-face interaction to cultivate and build the relationship.

Which means you may need to get on a plane (at your expense) and meet them in person.

While spending a few hundred dollars on travel, coffee or lunch may seem exorbitant, you need to weigh up the cost against the benefits they may be able to provide in terms of your company's growth objectives.

As you build a relationship and rapport with an influencer, think about how you can make it mutually beneficial. While the benefits their association can bring to your company are obvious, make sure they can also benefit.

How can your company support them? Their biggest motivation will probably be increasing their reach and status, so they'll appreciate you sharing their work with your customers, prospects and networks. You could:

- share their article, blogs and videos
- share news about upcoming events or initiatives the influencer is involved in
- provide access to industry experts, industry leaders, business colleagues and contacts you know the influencer would be interested in meeting.

There's no 'silver bullet' when it comes to working with influencers. Each one will want to engage with you and support your company in a different way. And they all have their own personalities and styles, which means you'll need to adapt your approach.

You'll also need to invest time (and sometimes money) to understand them, their subject matter domain and their perspectives on it. But it will help you build a mutually beneficial relationship that delivers positive outcomes for both parties and helps your company achieve its growth aspirations.

Chapter summary

The five areas of business innovation provide numerous ways for your business to innovate and drive growth through B2B markets. So you must examine your entire business closely (including your offerings, processes, strategies and business model) to identify the best innovation options for pursuing your company's growth objectives.

....

Take action now

Discuss the following questions with your management and cross-functional strategic planning teams to ascertain how your company could implement customer advocacy and influencer marketing programs.

Customer advocacy programs

- Who are the current clients/customers that really like what your company does?
- What should the goal of your company's customer advocacy program be?
- What strategies will be put in place to generate:
    - reviews
    - referrals
    - references
- How will you measure and manage the advocacy program?
- Do you currently have any customer reward programs or incentives set up? If so, how could they be improved or expanded to provide better participation?
- Do you know the types of rewards and recognition those raving fans would find valuable?

Influencer Marketing

- What could be potential goals for using influencers?
- Review your current LinkedIn contacts, colleagues and business networks. Get your management team and staff to do the same.
  - Does anyone have a relationship with any independent influencers or micro-influencers?
  - Which of them (if any) may be able to help your company with its goals?
  - Who else in your networks have you identified as an influencer or micro-influencer?
- What value could your company potentially offer them?
- What will be your initial plan of attack to reach out and establish contact with the potential influencers you identified?

CHAPTER 7

Developing a winning B2B strategy

Chapter overview

In the last chapter we talked about the four types of business innovation, and how you can apply them in a B2B context to meet the needs of your business customers and drive business growth.

In this chapter we look at strategy and answer four key questions:

- What is strategy?
- Why do startups and SMEs need a strategy?
- How can you develop your company's strategy specifically for B2B?
- How do you incorporate growth as part of your company's strategy?

It's a critical chapter, and one you'll keep referring to as you work through the rest of the book and run your business.

What is strategy?

Strategy is essentially a plan that provides the 'running sheet' for your company. An effective strategy provides clarity and focus to all members of your company as to what it will and will not do.

As Roger Martin and Al Lafley stated in *Playing to Win*, **strategy is ultimately about making explicit choices and then building a business around those choices**[40].

Why startups and SMEs need to have a strategy

Many business founders and senior leaders think developing a strategy is a time-consuming and often time-wasting exercise done primarily by large corporates. Many leaders of startups and SMEs don't develop any strategies for their business, and instead adopt lean startup approaches based on:

- developing hypotheses
- conducting experiments
- developing prototypes.

The lean startup methodology certainly has its benefits and applications (we discussed some of them in previous chapters). But here are a few reasons startups and SMEs operating in B2B still need a strategy.

1. Limited resources

Most startups and SMEs have limited:

- money
- skilled staff
- equipment
- access to distribution.

Taking advantage of growth opportunities in B2B markets often requires a large investment of money and other resources. Companies must conserve these resources and focus on whatever will give them the best chance of winning.

2. Decisions are interdependent

One department's projects and initiatives can affect other business units within the company. For example, when an IT firm's product or service development team creates a new training offering, they'll also need time and resources from the marketing, client services and HR teams.

Having a strategy will ensure that all areas of your company work together on the initiatives that will generate the greatest return on investment for the entire business.

3. Simple experiments aren't always feasible or useful in B2B

As we mentioned earlier, lean methodologies are based on experimentation. You create an offering, improve it, and test it in the market.

But while it may work for incremental improvements to an existing product, here are some B2B scenarios where this kind of testing isn't feasible.

- Radically new product and service offerings that need:
  - longer-term investments
  - significant involvement of multiple functions
  - suppliers and partners (potentially).

  In these cases, modifications and improvements could be both expensive and time consuming.

- B2B customers may need time to appreciate the value of your new product or service. For example, it may take months for a business owner to realize how well a firm's new analytic and reporting tools is helping their company achieve its objective.

Strategy provides a plan for achieving growth and profitability by linking forward thinking with day-to-day events.

Despite the importance of having a strategy to drive growth and profitability, strategic planning is a topic neglected by startups and SMEs. In Australia, only one in ten medium-sized firms have strategic plans[40]. Similarly, only 44% of SMEs in Canada have conducted a growth or strategic planning exercise in the past few years[41].

Benefits of an effective strategy

While an effective strategy takes effort to create, it will allow your company to:

- identify sustainable and profitable opportunities, and avoid pursuing opportunities that aren't suited to your company
- stay focused on 'where you can win' and avoid doing too much and spreading your resources too thinly. It will also ensure any experimentation and innovation is conducted within defined focus areas
- align the entire organization by empowering employees
- avoid duplicating efforts and pursuing conflicting agendas
- maintain a forward-thinking mindset that protects your business from obsolescence.

How strategy relates to listening and innovation

Strategy is about making choices regarding:

1. where to focus
2. how to win.

1. Where to focus

You can work out where to focus by listening to:

- yourself, your team, and your company in terms of its vision/ objectives, strengths and capabilities (the 'you' we discussed in Chapter 1)
- industry and geographic trends and characteristics, competitor activities and strengths (the 'market' we discussed in Chapter 2)
- current customers, previous customers and prospects (the 'customers' we discussed in Chapter 3).

2. How to win

By using various forms of business innovation you can determine:

- **what to deliver** by using product/service innovation
- **how to deliver** by using process and/or organizational innovation
- **how to promote** and engage by using marketing innovation.

How to develop your company's B2B customer-driven strategy

Time horizon for strategy development

In previous chapters we looked at McKinsey's *Three Stages of Growth* model as a framework for thinking about your innovation strategy and prioritizing activities.

To reiterate, it's important to think about strategy at different time horizons. The Three Stages model talks about stages defined by current and future revenue:

- Horizon 1: maintaining and defending core business
- Horizon 2: nurturing emerging business
- Horizon 3: developing ideas that comprise whole new businesses.

Given that most startups and SMEs have limited time and staff, and consumed by day-to-day operations, it's important to add a little reality to these horizons to suit the needs of SMEs. This will generally mean focusing on Horizon 1 and Horizon 2, where you get the biggest payoffs from investing in innovation.

Timeframe	Planning Objective	Key Considerations
Horizon 1 – short-term (up to 2 years)	Review Challenge the current strategy Evaluate progress Identify emerging issues and trends	Are you on track with the strategy? How do you adapt to changes in the business environment and emerging issues? What changes are needed to the plan?
Horizon 2 – medium-term (3-5 years)	Determine your B2B company strategy and corresponding initiatives needed to realize the company vision.	Which markets? Which customers? What to deliver? How to deliver? What innovation strategy? What capabilities?

In the next chapter we'll will discuss how to execute the strategy and regularly review and refine it.

Participants in the strategy development process

When you're developing your company's strategy, you should involve a range of people, including the company founders and representatives of key functional business units such as:

- finance
- human resources
- marketing
- operations
- product development
- sales
- customer service and support.

Some companies even involve customers.

As a general rule, anyone who will be executing the strategy should have a role in developing it—even if it's just providing feedback on what's been created. This is critical, as those who execute the strategy will know what's feasible and what potential issues, bottlenecks and other considerations should be addressed.

Your strategy team (if you have one) or a person in charge of business strategy will probably drive the strategic planning process. But they shouldn't develop the strategy in isolation. The more people you involve from different backgrounds, regions, generations and roles, the more ideas and perspectives you'll get and the more likely your business will succeed in an ever-changing and highly competitive business environment.

How to develop your B2B strategy

The key to developing an effective B2B company strategy for driving growth is to pull together your company's people and resources in a way that reflects your company's vision, strengths, capabilities and business customer needs.

B2B strategy development is about pulling together and documenting how your company can:

- leverage its strengths and capabilities
- leverage market opportunities
- plan the road map to achieve growth.

Developing your 3–5-year (Horizon 2) B2B company strategy consists of:

1. Synthesizing what you learned by listening to 'you', the markets and customers to know what industries, geographic markets and customers to focus on
2. Identifying the types of business innovations your company will undertake, based on the industries, markets and customers you're targeting

3. Determining what pathway you'll use to drive growth
4. Identifying the capabilities needed to execute your company's B2B strategy, and determining how any capability gaps will be filled
5. Identifying your plan to deliver and assigning resources to deliver over a specified time frame.

Let's look at the process in more detail.

Synthesizing what you learned by listening to 'you'

To know what industries, geographic markets and customers your company should focus on, you need to reconfirm your company's vision, mission and goals. You can confirm its overall direction by having the company's leadership team, business owners and Board (if applicable) discuss and agree on the company's future direction.

Once you have agreement on your company's strategic direction, you need to examine its performance to determine what markets and customers your company should focus on. As we discussed in Chapter 1, this will involve:

- analyzing key metrics for each industry and market your company operates in
- examining your company's key assets, skills and capabilities.

It will also involve reviewing feedback and key learnings from your annual company strategy review, which we'll talk about in the next chapter.

This company-level analysis can be done by your finance or strategy teams, or by the person responsible for driving the strategy development process. Business functions such as marketing, products, operations and customer service should also provide input.

Synthesizing what you learned by listening to the market

As part of your strategy development, you also need to compile and analyze your findings from listening to the market. As we discussed in Chapter 2, this will include an analysis of:

- the market performance of both current and prospective industries and markets
- key trends
- competitors.

By completing this analysis, you'll gain insights into:

- the most profitable industries and geographic markets on a growth trajectory (and worth pursuing)
- the trends your company can take advantage of and respond to
- how you can differentiate and position yourselves against your key competitors.

Synthesizing what you learned by listening to customers

Your strategy must be driven by a thorough understanding of the priorities, requirements, motivations, preferences and key stakeholders in the B2B buying process.

You can do this by collating and analyzing the feedback you got from customers using the methods discussed in Chapter 3.

Once you've finished analyzing the results from listening to 'you', the market and customers, we recommend conducting one or more strategic workshops to:

- review and discuss the results
- determine 'where to focus' (i.e. which industries, geographic markets and business customers your company will focus on).

Once you've determined 'where to focus', you should choose the types of business innovations your company will undertake based on the needs, behavior and trends in your target industries, markets and key customers. The business innovations you undertake may focus on:

- what to deliver (product or service innovation)
- how to deliver (process or organizational innovation)
- how to promote and engage with business customers (marketing innovation).

To identify the business innovations of focus, we recommend meeting members of your management team and selected staff members from various business units and functions to review and discuss:

- the analyses from the listening activities
- feedback from the quarterly innovation review meetings (which we'll discuss in the next chapter).

Addressing the role of growth in your B2B strategy

As growing your company is a specific goal, your B2B strategic plan should include how it will grow. You and your leadership team need to decide which growth pathways to pursue, which may include:

- enhancing your current product/service offerings or markets served
- expanding into new markets
- diversifying into new markets or industries
- developing offerings for existing or new markets.

But articulating your growth plan is only the first step in pursuing growth. To grow successfully your company must focus on key aspects such as scaling up, managing finances, people and culture. (We'll be discussing these in detail in the Grow section of the book.)

Given the limited resources of startups and SMEs, you and your leadership team must 'place your bets' carefully and focus on areas where your company is well positioned to play and win.

Determining your capabilities requirements and fulfillment strategy

You now need to determine what capabilities you need, based on the strategy you developed. You'll probably need:

- specific knowledge/expertise
- systems
- processes
- equipment.

The strategy you developed may need your company to develop new capabilities and strengths while still leveraging existing ones. If you found any capability gaps, you'll need to work out how to fill them.

How to build capability

When it comes to meeting capability requirements you essentially have three options—build, borrow or buy. But as you'll see, some of the options are also business innovations.

Build	<ul><li>Create new processes or systems internally (process innovation)</li><li>Co-creation with customers (process innovation)</li><li>Joint venture/strategic alliance with another organization, such as fellow startup, SME or large corporate (organizational innovation)</li><li>Training program implementations (organizational innovation)</li></ul>

Borrow	• Business loan, lease equipment, hire contractors/ contingent workers
Buy	• Hire new staff • Purchase systems/equipment • Outsourcing (organizational innovation) • Acquire or merge with another business that has complementary competencies

When you're determining how to fill these capability gaps, you'll probably need additional input from business departments/functions such as IT, HR, operations and finance.

Achieving agreement and alignment

Once you've identified:

- 'where to focus'
- the business innovations you'll undertake
- your desired growth pathway
- the capabilities you need

you should identify and prioritize the key actions needed to achieve the defined goals in a 3–5-year horizon. If possible, you should review and discuss them with:

1. any business units or individuals involved in its execution for input and feedback
2. the leadership team.

The B2B company strategy should be finalized, documented and communicated throughout the organization so everyone knows the company's goals and strategy, and their role in its execution.

Once this is done, the strategy can be implemented. (We'll discuss how it's actually done in the next chapter.)

A final note on growth and strategy development

Even if customer acquisition is a core component of your B2B strategy, you need to build long-term relationships so customers renew their contracts and spend more on your products and services. Especially when you consider the characteristics of many B2B industries—long-term contracts, big dollars, big risks, high levels of complexity and a reliance on referrals and references.

Even with well-developed strategies, your company's success will depend on how well you execute your plans and manage your customers. (We'll discuss ways of doing it effectively in the next chapter.)

Chapter summary

Your B2B company strategy is based on **listening**—understanding your company's mission, vision, strengths and capabilities. Based on that understanding is knowing how your company can innovate across one or more of:

- what it delivers
- how it delivers
- how it promotes and engages with customers

to grow your company with the path you've chosen.

To develop your company's B2B strategy you need cross-functional participation by staff at various levels to:

- determine the target industries, geographic markets and customers
- identify the innovation and growth strategies to undertake
- identify the capability requirements and fulfillment strategy.

Strategy development is an iterative process. You must continually review and revise your strategy to cater for:

- changing market trends
- competitor activities
- technology developments
- changes in business customer behavior and expectations.

Each iteration of the company's strategy should get buy-in from everyone involved in its execution.

You'll find details of how startups and SMEs such as Ikabo, the Bellissimo Law Group and Palladium Insurance manage their strategy development in the case studies section at the end of the book.

Take action now

1. Meet with your management team and ask yourselves the following questions:
   a. Are your company vision, mission and goals still valid?
   b. In terms of business customers,
      i. Do you have a clear customer-driven strategy?
      ii. Do you know where your company should focus?
   c. Are there any capability gaps?
2. Appoint someone to lead the strategic planning process
3. Assemble a cross-functional strategy team
4. Working with your assigned strategy lead, determine your company's strategic planning process including:
   a. dates for key workshops
   b. processes for:
      i. getting business unit feedback and buy-in
      ii. documenting and communicating the strategy across the business.

CHAPTER 8

Implementation: Putting your B2B strategy into action

Chapter overview

The last chapter demonstrated the importance of having a vision and a plan to get there that's driven by the markets and business customers you want.

But developing a strategy isn't enough. You need to execute it—quickly. In this chapter we'll address the following questions:

- What key elements need to be executed?
- How do you prioritize what your company should do first?
- How do you develop, implement and manage customer/account plans?
- How do you manage business innovation initiatives?
- How do you review and update company strategies?

The core elements of strategy execution

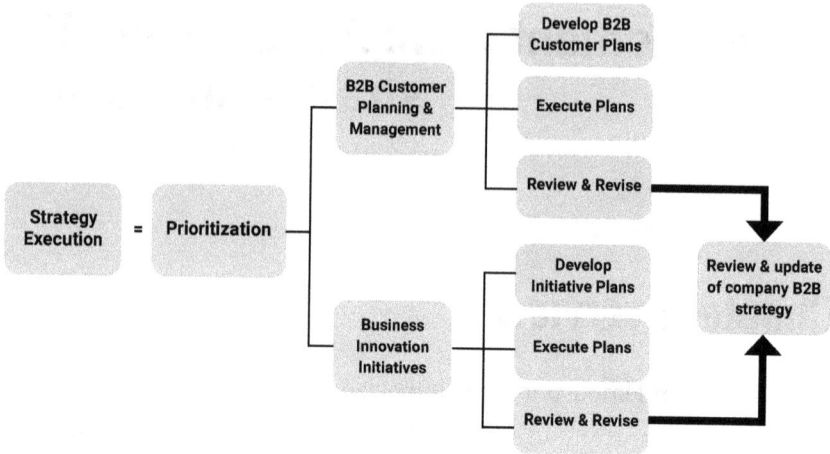

The Listen Innovate Grow Strategy Execution Framework

Strategy execution has two elements:

1. Prioritization

You and your management team need to prioritize at two levels:

- Customer-level planning and management: Developing customer plans for specific strategic prospects and customers
- Business innovation planning and execution: Specifying the business innovations to undertake and the resources and activities needed

2. Company strategy review and revision

Prioritization

Given your finite time and resources, you and your management team need to prioritize:

- the strategic prospects and customers your company will focus on

- the business innovation initiatives (e.g. process, product, service innovations) your company will focus on.

Criteria for selecting strategic customers and prospects

The following chart outlines the criteria for selecting customers and prospects to focus on.

You'll find the companies deemed critical to your growth are those you're highly aligned to in terms of your company's ability to *Listen, Innovate and Grow*.

Phase	Prospect/Customer Criteria
Listen	You have a strong understanding of the needs, objectives, challenges and goals of members of the buying group in this company. What you've 'listened' to (i.e. understood) aligns strongly to what you've 'listened' to about your company. In other words, you can attain what you want to be and achieve by aligning to and meeting their needs.
Innovate	As a result of deeply understanding these customers, you've identified opportunities to make improvements and/or develop entirely new: • products or services • processes • approaches to marketing and customer engagement. These satisfy both the needs of the strategic customers and your company's goals and objectives. These customers are willing/active participants in co-creating, testing and/or providing feedback on any innovations developed.

Grow	By meeting the needs of these customers, your company will achieve growth through one of more of the following: • revenues and repeat business earned directly from that customer • acquisition driven by referrals and recommendations • opening the door to new markets with product and service innovation.

Customer-level planning and management

For each strategic customer you choose to focus on, we recommend developing customer plans that detail how you'll provide value and engage with them to build strong relationships. It will give you clear and specific information on what mechanisms will increase acquisition, and help grow their spend with you.

To acquire and grow business customers, you need to create strong relationships with their buying group and decision makers. The more these customers:

- want what you can provide
- see your company as the best option
- believe you can produce and deliver

the stronger the relationship will be.

The key to achieving this is delivering value to each customer through two mechanisms:

1. **Value Connection:** Explore how you can provide more value to the client through your existing offerings
2. **Value Co-Creation:** Create new opportunities to deliver value through 'innovation' by working collaboratively with them[43].

To determine how your company can provide value to your customers and prospects, 'listen' to your customers using approaches such as strategic customer reviews, in-depth interviews and executive summits and forums.

Once you've 'listened' to your strategic customers and prospects, you can create customer plans detailing how you'll deliver value through product, service or process 'innovations'.

In the next section we'll discuss how to create B2B customer plans.

Managing your B2B customers and prospects

Once you've identified your most important customers and prospects, you need to manage them. One approach is to establish the three key customer/account management roles:

1. **The relationship lead:** This person (typically the account manager or business development manager) creates and strengthens the relationship and protects your company from competitors trying to infiltrate and win over your customers.

2. **The entrepreneur (aka 'the driver'):** This person (often the account manager or business development manager) leads the change for maximizing business within a customer account. It's a critical role—without it there's no-one to drive account growth and plans don't get built or implemented.

    But watch out. Many companies force the relationship lead into this role, and it often fails because the relationship lead doesn't have this skill set.

3. **The Technical Expert:** This person will have the relevant depth of knowledge and expertise in specific areas, and an ability to solve problems and facilitate discussions. If you don't have this person in your account team, your company chances to create growth and value may have limited, as many opportunities will probably get shot down[44].

You don't need a person for each role—they can all be filled by one or more people. What's important is to cover the key roles for each strategic customer or prospect.

Now that you've assembled your customer account teams, the next step is for them to create the B2B customer plans for your strategic customers and prospects.

The B2B customer plan

We recommend developing customer plans for each strategic customer and prospect so you and your teams have a clear road map of how to manage (and hopefully grow) these customers.

Key components of the B2B customer plan

The customer plans for your key strategic customers and prospects should be detailed and include the following:

1. **Overall competitive positioning**

Why our company?

2. **Your company's account goals**

These should be measurable and include:

- number of additional products and services purchased
- number of referrals/references
- increase in money spend
- contract renewals
- trials of new products/services (metric: number of trials conducted)
- collaboration/co-investment in innovation projects (metric: number of projects, money invested)

3. **Customer research**
- Company:
    - Organizational structure, ownership structure, markets/customers they serve, key developments

- Stakeholders:
    - Identification of buying group: buyers, users, influencers, change agents
- Objectives, priorities, key motivations and drivers of buying group:
    - Opportunities for strategies and actions
    - What opportunities to create value with existing offerings
    - What opportunities exist for business innovation to provide more value
        - Product, service innovation (co-creation)
        - Process innovation
        - Organizational
        - Marketing
    - Opportunities to penetrate other buying groups
- Client engagement and feedback plan:
    - Buyer engagement and feedback (e.g. strategic customer workshops/visits, forums)
    - User level feedback (e.g. operational/service reviews, surveys)
    - Schedule for customer plan reviews
- Key considerations:
    - Overall strengths
    - What is needed to strengthen the relationship?
    - What risks exist (or could exist) in the current relationship?

Important considerations for your B2B customer planning

For those customers who aren't high-priority strategic customers, you may want to develop high-level customer plans knowing they won't get the attention and focus of your key strategic accounts.

Whoever is responsible for managing your customers and prospects should work with representatives from across the company to develop the B2B customer plans. Try to get diverse views from various functional areas, departments and teams. You should also ask for feedback and input from your management team.

Customer plans should be developed iteratively in a series of workshops or meetings, and reviewed annually. Ideally, they should be done in alignment with your company strategy planning. This will ensure that what you focus on at a company level translates into how you manage and grow your strategic customers and prospects.

Quarterly reviews

When your account teams finish developing their customer plans for your key strategic customers, they can quickly be forgotten. The plans get put in the bottom drawer, and everyone gets on with business as usual.

To avoid this, we recommend that account teams meet regularly (quarterly or six-monthly) to discuss:

- progress on agreed business innovations
- developments and activities within the customers' organizations
- customer issues
- customer feedback obtained through customer meetings and visits, strategic customer reviews or discovery workshops during the quarter
- key actions and priorities for the next quarter

The learnings and outcomes from these customer review meetings can be fed back to your company's senior management team by either:

- those who attended the meeting
- the account team member in the 'value creator' role.

Priorities, actions, issues and customer feedback should also be documented and stored in a central repository or knowledge center so management and other departments can refer to it.

B2B customer management in action: Empower Construction

Empower Construction is an award-winning construction company that specializes in external cladding for residential and commercial properties.

Ryan Steyn (Empower's MD founder) and his team strongly believe in the importance of continuous improvement to meet the needs of their customers. To achieve this, staff conduct weekly site meetings with clients to discuss project progress and issues. Once completed they're reviewed and signed on-site with the builder.

They also conduct quarterly management meetings with key clients to discuss current issues and prevent future ones. Empower's founder also meets with the national and regional construction managers ('the buyers') every six months to understand clients' needs.

All feedback is captured via Google Forms and Asana, and given to Empower staff during company meetings. These meetings have an 'Identify-Discuss-Solve' segment to discuss and resolve client issues.

Business innovation planning and execution

Having completed your 'listening' activities and company strategy, you and your management team have probably identified numerous potential innovation opportunities. Now you need to prioritize which business innovation opportunities you should focus on and pursue.

To determine where your company should devote its time and resources, you'll need to establish a set of criteria to drive these decisions.

Criteria for evaluating and selecting innovation initiatives includes:

- alignment to company vision and strategic goals
- impact on company growth
- number of customers affected
- types of customers affected
- potential customer impact
- alignment to buyer needs
- timeframe required
- investment required
- complexity to implement
- facilities, equipment/machines and materials needed
- specialized knowledge/skills required
- number of staff required

To help you plan your initiatives we've provided an innovation checklist matrix at the end of the book (after the case studies).

It's important to get agreement on the prioritization criteria from all relevant business units and functions in the company.

You and the people you're collaborating with need to review and discuss the innovation initiatives being considered. And you and your management team will need to answer the following questions:

- What are the business innovation priorities (based on the agreed criteria)?
- In what order should the innovation initiatives be undertaken?
- Which innovations will get funding?
- What other initiatives are currently underway?
- Will trade-offs need to be made (e.g. other initiatives that need to be stopped for these prioritized initiatives to happen)?
- Who will own these agreed initiatives?

Once you've agreed on which innovation initiatives will proceed and appointed initiative leads, you'll need to start planning to get them underway.

But while there are hundreds of books on how to develop products or ideas and take them to market, here are the key steps you need to know.

Key steps in innovation initiative planning

- **Define the end state:** In every business, there's a danger the innovation won't deliver anything to the customer because the company is always trying to achieve perfection. The minimum viable product (MVP) needs a defined end state—characteristics and specifications that can be used internally and with prospective customers to describe what it does.

  A great way to define the product is to write 'user stories' that define:

  - what the product does
  - the benefit to the customer
  - the features that deliver those benefits
  - why it's an improvement on the current version.

  The end state may also define what the product is not as well as what it is.

- **Set your timelines:** Develop an overall project plan that identifies who will be working on the innovation project, what they will be contributing, and when. Identify any contingencies (i.e. things people will have to wait for before they can start their task) and ensure you're working towards an ultimate end state.

- **Document as you go:** Record the exact specifications of the capability or innovation so it has a defined scope. Typically, the documentation should be at a technical level that gives the people creating the new process or technology a clear set of instructions or recipe on how to build the desired product.

- **Check in:** To ensure you stay on track, have regular catch-ups with people working on the project to ensure everyone is working on their tasks and aligned in their progress. If you don't, you risk catastrophic issues such as:

- Products being built incorrectly
- Bottlenecks due to contingencies in the workflow not being understood
- Misunderstandings about the end state being sought.

Most check-ins these days are huddles with agile development principles.

- **Innovate incrementally:** Sometimes known as agile development, this is where you test and re-test features and performance throughout the initiative or project rather than when the innovation has been fully developed. It allows for variation to be built into the development process. (The initial solution design rarely captures or addresses requirements, which becomes clear as the concept is developed.)

- **Perform user acceptance testing (UAT):** Have a final UAT process to ensure what's being delivered meets the initial statement of requirements, scope and design. Despite your best intentions and regular check-ins, there will inevitably be variations in the design process that need remediation.

   By checking in at the end, you'll ensure you get the product you expected. If it's not what you expected, you'll have that last chance to make changes before you lock the cycle down into delivery.

Key steps in project planning

- **Form the project team:** The team will include a project manager to oversee and manage the project, along with the required members with the requisite skills and knowledge.

- **Develop the project plans:** These should include:

   - scope of the innovation initiative
   - goals and objectives (i.e. the end state to be achieved)
   - project timeline

- key project phases (e.g. building, user testing, capturing feedback)
- key activities within all key project phases
- key milestones
- team members
- assigned roles and responsibilities
- processes, steps and timing for collecting, discussing and circulating customer feedback
- project governance including:
  - schedule and timings for regular project team meetings and updates
  - required project documentation that must be completed at key phases (e.g. product build phase, user testing).

Each project team should meet regularly (weekly or fortnightly) to review, progress, identify and resolve issues. The outcomes of these meetings should be documented, centrally stored, and circulated to the B2B account teams and senior management so they know the progress of the initiatives and any potential implications.

Reviewing innovation initiatives

Evaluating your company's innovation initiatives shouldn't be a one-off process. As strategies, business customer needs and market conditions change and new opportunities emerge, you need to adjust accordingly. It's worth having a scheduled and formal process to review your current innovation initiatives, and discuss and evaluate new ones.

We recommend you and your management team meet with the leads of the innovation initiatives quarterly to discuss:

- progress and performance of the identified innovation initiative
- any issues raised from previous meetings
- any changes to the scope, budget or timing of any initiatives

- new developments (e.g. market conditions, customer needs, new trends)
- any proposed new initiatives
- which (if any) new initiatives will receive approval and funding
- key activities/next steps for innovation initiatives in the coming quarter.

All decisions and discussions should be documented and centrally stored for future reference. And the outcomes of these meetings should be communicated to the account teams so they can adjust their customer plans if necessary. They also should be incorporated into, and discussed at, the annual company strategy planning/review meetings.

Balancing innovation with the disciplines of growth

As you can see, good processes help you develop innovation as a structured part of your business. But we need to warn you about some of the trade-offs you'll face when advancing innovation in your business. These involve linking innovation (and the choices of where to innovate) with the likely payoff in growth in its various forms, and ultimately revenue and profit.

To ensure you're innovating in the right areas, you need to understand these costs and how they align with your company's goals and mission.

Ultimately, all innovation activity in your business must tie-in with what your business does best.

The paradox of being strategic versus being opportunistic

Being customer-driven means being able to 'listen' and identify innovation opportunities.

But opportunities often come up that force you to reassess your existing commitments.

These innovation opportunities may not be tied to revenue opportunities. Choosing *not* to prioritize them or take them can lead to opportunity costs as competitors jump in and fulfill them.

During your innovation review process, you must consider the broader and longer-term effects on the customer relationship.

When innovations are quick and easy, and have revenue-earning potential, not rejigging your existing innovation pipeline to take them on can result in a real opportunity cost in foregone revenue. So you must examine such innovation opportunities closely, and consider them during your scheduled review process.

There's no easy answer to this paradox. All you can do is clearly understand the future benefit of your existing work program (and each item in it) to be able to make rational decisions about priority and order. You should conduct a financial analysis of all potential opportunities as part of your strategy review and planning processes.

Moving your team from one project to another also has its problems as it can interrupt focus. The danger is you end up with unfinished or unrealized projects.

Annual company strategy review and planning session

Given all the activities your company is undertaking in terms of managing your key strategic customers and your innovation initiatives, it's important to review your company's strategies every year.

The purpose of the annual company strategy review and planning session is to discuss the company's annual and three-year strategic plans in light of the company's performance during the year. You should also review any new developments that may have occurred, such as:

- emerging trends/new technologies
- changing market conditions
- changing business customer needs and behavior
- new opportunities (e.g. new markets, innovation opportunities)

When mapping the future direction and priorities of the company, it's worth getting all relevant stakeholders to participate in the sessions including:

- founders
- your management team
- B2B customer account team representatives, particularly those in the 'driver' and 'value creator' roles
- innovation initiative leads
- strategy team or strategy lead (if applicable in your company)

Topics you should discuss in these sessions include:

- review of performance versus established goals
- strategic accounts and their performance
- innovation initiative progress and performance
- market, industry and competitor developments and trends, including new/emerging disruptors, technologies and business models

- customer needs and buying behavior
- new opportunities
  - customers
  - markets
  - innovation opportunities
- clarification of strategic direction
- strategic goals and priorities
- key strategic initiatives
- confirmation of metrics

For SMEs with a more formal organizational structure, you need to communicate the strategic direction, goals, priorities and next steps you agreed to throughout the organization. Each manager should communicate what it means for their respective departments and teams so everyone knows the 'So what?' for them. This may be done by circulating a one-page strategy summary, providing the details on your company intranet and/or conducting 'town hall' meetings.

Annual strategy review and planning in action: The Bellissimo Law Group (BLG)

The Bellissimo Law Group (BLG) is an immigration law firm based in Toronto, Canada, that specializes in complex immigration appeals and inadmissibility cases.

At BLG, the annual strategy review and planning is done by the firm's founder, Mario Bellissimo, and the leads of the firm's six core departments:

- Procedures
- Litigations
- Admissions

- Communications
- Accounting/Administration
- Legal Research, Writing and Publications.

The process begins with a compilation of the company's current strategic plan, financials, client audits and list of referrals. Mario and the department leads review and discuss this data, and an initial draft strategy of 1-2 pages is prepared in point form.

Meetings are conducted with various teams across the departments to both brief them on the proposed strategy and its rationale, and to get their feedback. They get written feedback from both the department leads and their respective teams, which is then reviewed by Mario and the department leads.

The strategy is refined if it's deemed necessary, and then it's circulated across the organization to ensure buy-in, which Mario believes is critical to implementation.

Strategy planning and execution isn't a one-off process at BLG. Mario continually asks for ongoing feedback through both the weekly team meetings and the bi-monthly all staff meetings.

As a result, the firm's strategy is continually being refined as needed.

Chapter summary

Prioritization is a key step in strategy execution, and is achieved by identifying:

- the customers and prospects your company will focus on
- the types of business innovations you 'll undertake.

You select each one using a series of criteria pertaining to:

- the business customers' needs and their alignment to your company goals and capabilities
- being able to identify and undertake business innovations that meet both customer needs and company goals
- the effect on driving your company's growth.

Once you've prioritized your customer and innovation opportunities, your account teams will create B2B customer plans for each of your target prospects and key customers. These plans should detail:

- how your company will deliver value through your existing offerings
- the innovation initiatives your company will undertake
- how your company will engage with key stakeholders.

Because business customer needs and market conditions change, and new trends emerge, you should review both your B2B customer plans and the innovation initiatives being undertaken regularly (we suggest quarterly) to ensure your company is:

- focusing its resources
- managing and engaging its customers appropriately.

We also recommend reviewing and updating your company strategy regularly to ensure it takes into account:

- changing business customer needs
- changing market conditions
- new market or innovation opportunities
- emerging trends.

You should get cross-functional input for all changes and updates to the B2B customer plans, innovation projects and company strategy. And then you need to communicate them throughout the company so everyone knows what the company is striving for, and the role they play in it.

Take action now

Compile a list of your current key prospects and strategic customers.

Meet with your management and customer account teams and assess each key prospect and strategic customer using the LIG prospect/customer criteria. As you go through them, ask yourselves:

- Do we have a deep understanding of the buying decision-makers and their needs, priorities, drivers and buying behavior?
- Are our current offerings still delivering value to these strategic customers and prospects? What 'value gaps' exist?
- How have they affected the company's performance in terms of sales, referrals, references and case studies?

Compile a list of innovation initiatives that are planned or already underway:

- Identify which of these (if any) could meet the needs of the key strategic customers and prospects your company will focus on.
- Could other business innovations meet any unmet needs? (Remember to consider all four types of business innovation.)

PART 3

GROW by aligning your business operations

Section overview

At this point in our *Listen, Innovate, Grow* journey we've discussed how the growth planning process starts with listening— to 'you', your customers and the market. We then looked at how to implement your business planning results so you can drive growth opportunities in your company by knowing where and how to innovate.

The final section of this book is about making sure your company is ready and able to grow. We'll review:

- **Capability growth:** How you need to review your business periodically to address bottlenecks and reform your capabilities to effectively manage a growing business.
- **Financing Growth:** How to effectively manage the flow of money from customers to your accounts and invest it into your growth activities.
- **People and Growth:** The critical role your team and employees play in driving your success, including creating a culture that:
  - facilitates growth
  - helps you find and retain the right talent
  - avoids the problems associated with larger teams of people.

By reviewing these three areas you'll:

- know where and how to innovate to unlock growth
- ensure your company makes the most of this growth by scaling up efficiently.

CHAPTER 9

....

Growth pathways

....

Chapter overview

Now that we've defined how to develop and implement a B2B customer-driven strategy for growth, it's time to consider how to actually achieve that growth.

This isn't the same as unlocking growth through customer-led innovation, which is the book's core focus. We're referring to the underlying mechanisms that increase your business income when you enact the strategies we discuss in the book.

This is important because you need to know how your innovations are driving growth, and how it could affect your broader strategy (e.g. opportunity and risk).

Each growth pathway has its own characteristics and implications. Knowing the pathway you're on gives you the knowledge and insight to be an effective growth manager—someone who has the skills for growth and knows how to align the business to grow successfully.

What are growth pathways?

There are only so many way to grow your business. And we think of them as growth pathways because they're like the fundamental outcomes of all growth strategies and plans.

The four pathways to growth are:

1. **Growing your overall market** – bringing new users to your product or service category, or persuading those already active in your market to spend more and/or more often.
2. **Increasing market share** – taking more of what's currently bringing in spend in your addressable market (i.e. the spend of all potential buyers of your product of service).
3. **Price increases** – increasing the price of your product or service so that the overall revenue increases.
4. **Extensions** – undertaking new business endeavors based on identified market and customer opportunities.

For each pathway, the key is innovation, which we believe arises from truly knowing your customers.

Let's look at each growth pathway in more detail.

Pathway 1: Growing your overall market

Every business owner wants to operate in a growing market because it means you can grow just by standing still. (As the saying goes, 'A rising tide lifts all boats.') If the market you operate in grows by 20%, you'll enjoy the benefits of that growth without having to increase your market share or spend.

But tides ebb and flow, and relying on market growth alone will probably end in trouble for your business. A competitor will inevitably innovate, which will disrupt your market, undermine your competitiveness and diminish your customer appeal.

When that happens, your business may become a declining player in a growing market – a market that no longer resembles the one you thought you were competing in. Worse still, the innovation may be so disruptive that it makes your whole category irrelevant. This is the so-called 'Kodak moment', coined by the company's inability to foresee the shattering impact digital photography would have on its business.

If entering a growing product or service market is your goal, you need to ask yourself a deeper and more important question: "How do I make sure I'm keeping pace?" It requires constant vigilance on where things are heading in your category and a willingness to be ahead of trends, or at least be an early adopter.

In the long run, staying still is accepting defeat.

Growing through overall market growth doesn't need to be a passive strategy. Cooperate with your competitors to gain mutual growth, and engage with industry bodies such as:

- chambers of commerce
- advocacy and lobby groups funded by your industry.

These bodies are set up to promote a particular industry or market to achieve mutual benefit.

Pathway 2: Increasing your market share within your market

Increasing market share means capturing a greater share of sales from your competitors within your addressable market (i.e. the sum total of companies that could buy what you produce).

While growing market share is the pinnacle of success, it can put particular stresses on your business. You must grow your operational capabilities to support and deliver to your increasing customer patronage. This can lead to the challenges we mentioned in the previous chapter— less personal time, more costs, and a need to change how you run your day-to-day business operations.

Growing your market share implies your business is doing something better than your competitors, because customers prefer you to the alternatives. But it can also mean your prices are too low, and people are using you because they're getting a better deal than they can get from anywhere else. You're delivering superior value through the price lever, and giving away value to gain market share.

In a supplier–buyer relationship, value gets shared by the mechanism of price. If you price too low, you're effectively 'buying' the relationship and giving customers more than their fair share. If you price too high, you're choosing to retain more of the value for yourself, albeit at the potential cost of relationships and lower sales.

Some strategies for increasing market share aren't based on innovation—promotional pricing, effective sales and marketing, and development of superior distribution channels. Unfortunately, these are outside the scope of this book. But it's worth noting that customer-led innovation can be applied across all these areas, as we'll see in the next section of the book.

You may deliberately choose to grow your market share by reducing your prices or loss-leading. It's a valid strategy, especially for developing new relationships you normally wouldn't be able to establish due to incumbency. But only do it if you expect to be rewarded with service delivery at a sustainable level of profit. Everyone plays the game of using competitive tendering to reduce prices and keep suppliers 'honest'. If you deal with corporate sourcing as part of your buying cycle then it's probably a key (and possibly counter-productive) focus.

Watch out – winner's curse

Winner's curse is where the winning bid at an auction implicitly exceeds the value of the item purchased. The only person willing to pay that much for the item is the winner.

The same logic can be applied to a competitive tender situation where a buyer wants to improve the value they're getting from their suppliers.

If you're the 'in' supplier (i.e. you're the incumbent), you'll have the full details of what the contract needs to fulfill. But if you're the 'out' supplier (i.e. you're tendering to win the contract from the incumbent), you only have whatever information the buyer is willing to share.

Unfortunately, buyers often write tender documents that are insufficient or leave out critical details the 'in' buyer has already factored into their quote.

The danger is that if you're the 'out' tenderer, and you agree to deliver the product or service for the lowest amount to win the tender, you'll be 'cursed' by your success.

It's easy to be caught up in the thrill of the chase, with a win-at-all-costs mentality. But the exhilaration of winning can quickly be replaced by the realization that you've done something that will cause a lot of grief, and potentially limit your company's growth potential.

Pathway 3: Increasing revenue by increasing prices

If we define increasing revenue as growth, then a pathway to growth is to increase prices. But as you know, it's not that simple in practice.

There's a fundamental economic relationship between price and demand. Most markets are elastic—increasing prices decreases demand. In this situation, the pricing sweet spot is where revenue is maximized because demand matches supply. The same principle applies whether it be:

- an hourly rate in a consulting company
- unit costs in a manufacturing company
- the rack prices of an importer or wholesaler.

A second reason pricing is important for growing businesses is that growing businesses consume more cash than stable businesses do. As we saw previously, new contracts and supply arrangements cost money to establish. So growing by winning lots of new business will consume cash reserves (at least in the short term). Unless you front-load contracts, your profits will decrease.

This suggests that a growing business should focus on lowering its acquisition and customer establishment costs.

As you can see, pricing is an important consideration in growth. And you need to understand the value of your product and price your innovations accordingly. But with so many books on pricing we won't go into any more detail than the key concepts we just introduced.

One more point we'd like to make on pricing and growth relates to businesses with commodity products and services, or in highly liquid markets (i.e. where customers can easily move supplier). You may be producing textiles for shoes, and your competitor produces exactly the same textile. Or perhaps you provide a business loan where there's no exit cost and the interest rate is exactly the same.

If your company is in this situation, it means your customers are highly transactional and can easily go somewhere else to get the same product or service. You need to avoid this situation. Innovation is one way to get out of this trap.

Here are the key points to following the price pathway to growth:

- Increasing prices generally decreases volume unless your customers are willing to pay more than they are today.

- There's a pricing sweet spot that maximizes profit, but you generally won't know what it is. If you underprice you won't get the most for your inputs, and if you overprice you'll have unused capacity/resources.

- Growing costs money because:

  - you need to invest in new processes and systems
  - there's a cost of winning new contracts.

- You should avoid competing on price. (We can't say this enough.)

Here are tips for effective pricing:

1. Where possible, price a little higher than what you're comfortable with. But let buyer know you'll discount if necessary.

2. Avoid underpricing your offer. It devalues your offering and makes it harder to raise your prices later.

3. Consider rack pricing tiers (i.e. different offers at different prices) so your customers can select the price and level of delivery/quality that suits them.

4. Don't share your pricing on your website. It gives your competitors the information they need to price competitively. You can instead offer an 'enterprise' tier with 'price on application', which lets you decide how to price according to the most valuable opportunities.

Pathway 4: Extension

To grow your business, you must think beyond what your business does today. If you don't, the result will be something we've mentioned previously, Theodore Levitt's **marketing myopia**, (i.e. when businesses define what they do too narrowly, they risk market obsolescence). To grow, companies need to listen to, act on and exploit the needs and desires of their customers[42].

The underlying concept is that the needs of customers change and shift over time due to:

- the collective impact of exposure to new and better ways of doing things
- their own internal changes
- actions to compete in their markets.

The key implication for you is to define what you do broadly.

Watch out – Cost of entry

The overall value of a commercial opportunity is the net value of future earnings less the cost of entry. Common pitfalls for B2Bs and SMEs on the market share growth pathway is **underestimating that cost of entry**.

Establishing a B2B supply relationship costs money. Preparing and submitting a proposal or tender takes time, and sometimes money. Getting your supply process up and running (re-machining your production line, writing contracts, developing documentation and processes, etc.) also takes time and money. So make sure you include these costs into your bid, especially if the contract includes exit clauses that could leave you out of pocket if the customer walks away.

The lesson here is to ensure you factor in the cost of entry when deciding where and how to increase your market share by attacking new and additional opportunities in your industry. Here are some critical questions to ask:

1. **How much effort is involved?** If the opportunity is in your sweet spot (something you're great at, and that will take relatively little effort to deliver), then it must carry a premium over potentially more lucrative opportunities with opposite characteristics.

2. **What are your chances of winning?** A key factor here is whether the opportunity is new to market or a repurchase. If it's the latter, how settled is the 'in' provider?

3. **Can you reduce the cost of entry?** Can you lower the cost of entry by developing a more efficient tender response process (e.g. developing information or response templates)? Once again, multi-tenanting is a critical concept to understand.

As an aside, if *you* are the 'in' provider, you should do everything possible to increase the cost of entry for other providers. The best way to do that is to be innovative. Be creating new ways to deliver products and services, or increase your efficiency, you make it harder for others to compete.

Chapter summary

Once you start listening and innovating, you need to consider how you'll grow. Growth pathways give you an insight into the way you're growing, so you can plan accordingly. They also give you an opportunity to think about whether you can grow your business in other ways.

Growing strategically means being mindful of the pathways you're on and aligning your pricing, product, marketing and sales strategies to maximize your growth opportunities.

Take action now

- Understand your growth. What pathway or pathways are you on?
- Understand your pricing. Will increasing prices decrease revenue and increase profit?
- Engage with industry bodies to increase compliance costs and hence barriers to entry. This is a particularly good strategy if you're in an industry that's relatively immature.
- Spend a day considering extension opportunities. Define your core competencies, and consider whether you can create new products that use your capabilities in new ways.

CHAPTER 10

Managing growth

Chapter overview

In this chapter we'll look at the stages a company goes through as it grows using the principles of listening and innovating.

The core principle is that growing companies hit pressures that can curtail that growth, and small and growing businesses need to change over time so their growth opportunities aren't strangled by weak structures or inadequate capabilities.

We'll present four generic stages of growth—starting up, forming, spreading and corporatizing. At each stage we'll look at the pressures that may arise, and what can be done to overcome them and progress to the next stage.

Stages of growth

If you grow your revenue without transforming your company, you'll feel pressure caused by the mismatch between your delivery capabilities and the demands placed on you by your expanded client base. The systems and capabilities you put in place were designed for a smaller business, and unsuitable for a larger business.

If you don't address these pressures, your business will stagnate. It may even trigger a crisis that could hold your company back, or even put it at risk.

The idea of constraints and stresses stagnating growth has been around for a long time. A large body of research has identified discrete stages growing companies move through. These stages are punctuated by periods of growth and stagnation. And when a business plateaus it needs to change so it can transcend the constraints limiting its growth, typically through some form of transformation.

This is referred to as a 'decision point'. And not recognizing these decision points (and adapting to the new challenges through transformation) is a primary cause of business failure.

Many models and frameworks describe growth stages and the key stresses and transformations that occur to overcome them. Based on our experience and the interviews we've conducted, we believe there are four identifiable stages. And while every business has a unique trajectory, it's still worth conceptualizing these stages and how they relate to your business.

Here's a summary of each stage:

Stage	Characterized by	Pressures	Transforming changes
Stage I: Starting up Typically 1-10 people	Individual or partners Startup mentality Excitement / high energy Naivety / inexperience Hands-on owners Limited funds Unstructured roles Flexibility Individual decision making	Production rates Quality control Lead times Cash flow Owner time Control	Start hiring people to do specific things, particularly dealing with clients Introduce processes to the business Create stronger financial disciplines

Stage	Characterized by	Pressures	Transforming changes
Stage II: Forming Typically 10-30 people	Larger but unstructured group Unclear reporting lines Can-do mentality – everyone pitches in Sense of purpose and mission – shared goals Still flexible but also slightly chaotic	Long owner hours Poor hiring decisions Quality control Trying to satisfy clients without focusing	Hiring specialist managers e.g. general manager Organizational structure defined Deciding where to play Documentation of processes Formal client feedback channels
Stage III: Spreading Typically 30-100 people	Professional management Standardized processes Growing economies of scale Efficiency focus Inward and outward organization Formal marketing and sales focus	Bureaucracy Red tape Hierarchical decision making Cultural change	Organizational restructure Review Mission and Vision Merger or acquisition Identify new growth channels

Stage	Characterized by	Pressures	Transforming changes
Stage IV Corporatizing Typically 100+ people	Expanding product range Experienced expert managers Renewing technology and formal product lifecycle management Actively looking for new growth opportunities Geographic expansion	Loss of purpose Losing innovation edge People leave to become competitors	Periodic review Rest and reflection Organizational revitalization

Our review of growth plateaus is a mix of different approaches to the basic concept of business stages and plateaus. The key takeaway from these models is to:

1. understand the status and stage your business is operating at
2. be prepared to enact change to overcome the pressures that arise.

It's vital for building on the listen and innovate stages.

Stage 1: Starting up

Key characteristics

In the traditional sense of the term, startups are companies at the beginning of their journey. We've observed various motivations for founders starting their business—pursuing a great idea to make a fortune, escaping corporate life, gaining control of their destiny, and even by accident.

But while the circumstances and motivations may vary, they all share some common factors such as:

- **High motivation:** The founder (or founders) are super focused and motivated about their new enterprise. It's an exciting time, with positive energy sustaining them through late nights and early mornings as their concept moves to reality and the new business takes shape. It's a period of uncertainty, but also of promise and potential.

- **Limited funds:** While it's not always the case, most startups start their journey with little or no cash flow. The business may be funded by capital investment, borrowings or savings. It's also common for a few foundation clients to be critical to its viability. During this phase, the 'burn rate' (i.e. how quickly you expend your starting capital before reaching the point where revenues outweigh costs) is critical. The story of internet unicorns being started in garages reflects an underlying reality. Cost-control is critical at this stage, and being frugal is a virtue. Limited funds need to be spent wisely, and every dollar needs to be accounted for.

  Few business owners should expect to be taking money out of the business at this stage. It's a common theme in all our interviews with successful high growth business founders. They all tightened their belts and did it hard for years until the business was viable.

- **Small number of people:** Most startups begin with only one or two people. This means the founders need to become a Jack (or Jill) of all trades. Many people find working on all aspects of the business both a challenge and a burden.

  But people still reminisce fondly about their startup experiences—the challenges, the learning curve, the chance to think outside the square—because so many things are being done for the first time with a fresh pair of eyes. The business founders are generally working on things they love and do best—one of the reasons they started the business in the first place.

- **Unstructured:** A hallmark of the startup is the absence of structure. After all, it's hard to have structure when only a few people are doing everything. But this lack of structure can be both a blessing and a curse. It can be a core enabler of innovation because the business has no legacy costs for change, and the environment is conducive to finding new ways of doing things. But the lack of people to delegate to means the founders must maintain innovation and drive change. If changes aren't made to delegate mundane responsibilities, there's little time left for creative thinking and working on the business.

Startup pressures

We won't bother you with the statistics. The truth is, most startups fail. A lot of them fail because of a lack of revenue or additional absence of cash flow. If the business can't manage its costs, or grow its top line faster than its bottom line, it will probably fail. Even if it doesn't, the opportunity cost of earning a pittance for long hours without any leave is huge.

Many businesses never grow beyond this stage. They've developed a profitable business, but the desire (or the know-how) to expand simply isn't there.

But most business do expand, and often face these pressures as demand increases and they take on more people.

- **Production pressures increase:** For a manufacturing company, increasing demand lead to increasing orders and a backlog, which in turn lead to delays and dissatisfied customers who may go elsewhere. Even in an efficient production line, this increase in demand can slow production due to bottlenecks—particularly if there's increased need for product variations driven by customers looking for more customization.

- **Quality control can suffer:** The lack of structure in a typical startup can lead to issues with quality control—consultancies preparing reports without adequate proofing, shopping companies losing orders, shipping companies missing deadlines. Quality control issues lead to expensive rework and dissatisfied customers who may find another supplier.

In the worst cases, a vicious cycle forms. Productivity spirals down because of the amount of time spent dealing with faults and quality issues—time that should be spent generating income or improving the business. It's important to recognize this cycle when it occurs, and find ways to break out of it.

- **Longer lead times:** Limited resources, and not keeping pace with demand, can create production delays. People start working in the evenings and on weekends to get things done, undermining job satisfaction and causing quality issues. No-one wants to work in a company where things feel out of control, so people start leaving. The extended lead times create customer dissatisfaction, resulting in cancelled orders and lost future business due to a lack of goodwill.

- **Constrained cash flow:** The other immediate and critical effect of extended lead times is reduced cash flow. You can't charge customers for orders you haven't filled.

  As we've noted several times, growing costs money. Explosive growth can lead to cash flow shortages as scarce capital is invested to increase capacity. You also have to contend with:

  - the need to invest in more machinery, people or support processes
  - time and money spent fixing problems
  - loss of income due to delayed order processing.

- **Pressures on owners:** Frenetic growth and no clear delegation structures can have company founders working long hours over an extended period, which leads to exhaustion and burnout.

  If you think you can work effectively on only a few hours' sleep you're kidding yourself. While many new business owners work long hours and wear it as a badge of pride, the reality is that exhaustion can lead to lower productivity, more mistakes and a loss of motivation.

What to do

Things can come to a head when the founders acknowledge that the company's growth means they'll have to fundamentally change the way things work. It can happen suddenly, or in small steps over time. Either way it can be emotionally difficult, particularly for those who are hands-on in the business and really love what they do.

The key steps to get past this stage are:

- **Hire specialists:** As the founders start considering the purpose and goals of the company, they realize it can't achieve its potential unless they change roles. They need to relinquish control, and hire specialists who can operate machines, write proposals, price properties, model data, etc.

  While it depends on the business, the most commonly people hired at this stage are 'doers'—sales people, account managers, consultants, machine operators and administrative staff. With the advent of contingent working, there are plenty of choices.

- **Introduce financial disciplines:** Financial controls are put in place to forecast revenue and profits, which in turn helps with business planning. It's a key innovation enabler, as it provides the disciplines to invest income in growth. (We'll look at taking control of your finances later in the book.)

  This is a critical step to enabling growth, and one of the key reasons businesses don't make it to the next stage.

- **Introduce processes:** Most businesses start out with limited or weak processes (if they have any processes at all).

  (By 'process' we mean treating the business as an input > process > output system, with each task in the system defined and documented.)

  Process is a two-edged sword. On the one hand, it ensures consistency and delivers redundancy by allowing people to take over a task when the primary person is sick, on leave or otherwise absent. It also defines what the business does, and creates a recipe to help everyone understand what the business does and how it does it.

On the other hand, documenting processes takes time. The myriad of ways things are done can create a level of complexity that's difficult to describe, let alone document. It can also stifle creativity. After all, if every business followed its defined processes, nothing would ever change.

But on the whole, process is a crucial foundation that supports many other facets of business organizational growth—particularly when more and more people become involved in how the business operates.

Getting the balance right between stability and change through innovation is the key to managing this phase. While process creates stability, innovation is the key to continued differentiation. Differentiation will drive higher prices and faster growth.

Process innovation will help you scale up in ways that don't rely on hiring more people, such as developing processes that allow for embedded change and improvement in how things are done. Whenever you're thinking of hiring someone, ask yourself, 'Can we deliver this by changing our process or being more efficient, rather than adding a new person?'

While being a startup is a crazy and exhilarating experience, it can't last forever if you have serious growth ambitions. Enjoy it while it lasts, but be ready for change.

Tips for managing growth in the startup phase

1. Look for the telltale signs that you need to transform:

    - A sharp increase in revenue, to the extent that you lose track of how much money you're making (or not making)
    - Not enough hours in the day to get everything done
    - Growing lead times, and taking longer to get things done
    - Customers grumbling about how long things are taking, or high rates of defection despite a high win rate.

2. Watch for common mistakes people make in this stage:

- Getting up earlier and going to bed later to get through a 'busy period' that never seems to end
- Resisting investing in people
- Random hiring without thinking about the long-term needs of the business or who will survive and thrive in a high-growth business
- Not retaining cash to invest in people and processes
- Not keeping customers informed about growth or providing a clear narrative on how the business is investing in resources to maintain quality
- Getting 'high' on success without being sober about the future.

Stage 2: Forming

Key characteristics

At this stage, your company is hiring more people. And for the first time, you'll have some of them reporting to other people.

In many ways this is the make-or-break point for growth. The 'magic' number where businesses start to struggle is around 20 employees. At this stage you need to change how you operate and adjust to a different reality in your business. (It's why this stage is called 'forming'—it's what you need to do to escape the trap of organized chaos.)

You need to create a business structure that works with a larger body of people. Some employees will no longer have a direct relationship with you.

Growth typically continues at a frenetic pace, and keeping the business growing to meet the demand can be challenging. (The 'spreading' stage is all about people, processes and creating sustainable systems to create structure and capability.) Key characteristics of this stage include:

- **Increased focus on people:** Before this stage, the small band of people in your business focused on its customers. But now that focus needs to shift towards your own people. You can't expect to run a business with more than a dozen employees without them consuming more of your time. It's time to face the reality of being a people manager.

- **Feeling of chaos:** As you spend more time running the business, dealing with people and servicing a growing customer base, it can sometimes feel like you're out of control. Dealing with this feeling without losing your cool is a challenge for you as a leader.

- **Unclear responsibilities:** When you only have a few people in your business, the lines of responsibility are clear. And it's easy for people to collaborate to solve problems. But once your numbers hit critical mass you need to start thinking more carefully about your organizational structure. The structure of your business will influence how it operates.

- **Client-based expansion:** Ideally, you'll be growing your clientele to mitigate risk. This means you should develop a clear client servicing structure to handle your customer relationships. You'll also need to start thinking about marketing and formalizing your processes to gain and manage clients.

Forming pressures

The key pressures at this stage are about people, processes and time. The company founders often feel it more because they're the ones who need to look at their methods and ways (and even change them if necessary), which can be confronting.

- **People issues arise:** If there's one defining characteristic of this stage, it's that you'll be spending more of your time dealing with people and their issues. When you get to around a dozen people, the dreaded 'office politics' can enter the workplace.

- **Quality takes a hit:** If you bring new people on board without strong documented processes in place, quality will inevitably suffer. You'll also have less time to focus on customers, and you'll have to hand over the reins to others.

  This transition process can be difficult. But while quality costs money, it's an investment you shouldn't be afraid to make.

- **Need to focus:** With new people and customers on board, you'll be tempted to try and do everything yourself. But as we discussed earlier, there's a fine line between being positively client led and being led into places you don't want to go and that have limited returns. Investment in capability should be guided by the return on investment, not only with your immediate client but also the broader market.

What to do

At this stage, the key is to specialize and delegate. This means you'll have people working on the business (working with your people, creating processes, coordinating effort, etc.) instead of with clients.

As the company owner, your role will also change. You'll need to consciously think about where you can add the most value, and that may not be running a small business. As always, get help and advice from someone you trust.

- **Develop strong budget processes:** At this stage, you'll hopefully be making some money. What you do with that money matters a lot. Suffice to say, cash flow gives you choices in what you do, who you hire and where you focus. Treat every dollar you earn with respect and watch costs closely. But don't be afraid to invest in capability to get the most out of your people and resources.

- **Create strong hiring processes:** It's often said that one of the hardest things about starting a business is finding good people. At this stage, finding good people is critical because they're joining at a time where every decision can have consequences. While you can use traditional recruiting sites or even LinkedIn, we've found that using your own networks and recommendations can be a great way to find people. (Later in the book we look at people in more detail, and consider the traits they need to succeed in a growth business.)

- **Formalize your organizational structure:** In a growing company, jobs can change with the business—sometimes quite abruptly. Nonetheless, you must ensure all your people, especially the new ones, have a clearly defined role so they know the boundaries they're operating in.

  The ultimate outcome of defining roles is to understand where everyone sits and who they work with. Most businesses, especially small and lithe ones, aim for flat structures where teaming up takes precedence over vertical reporting lines.

- **Apply the core principles around customer listening:** At this point in your growth curve it's easy to lose your customer focus. You'll spend more time with your own people so they can do their jobs and contribute to the success of the business.

  But some of them won't have first-hand contact with customers, which means you need to embed 'listening' to customers, and ingesting and capturing customer feedback, within the fabric of your business.

  More than ever, it's time to apply the ideas and concept of this book.

Tips for managing growth in the forming phase

- Engage a technical writer to help document your processes.
- Update your website regularly to capture case studies of new customers, and communicate your capabilities as they grow.
- Get an IT consultant to review your technical environment and develop a strong intranet with workplace social platforms such as Slack.
- Choose a CRM platform and develop a strong pipeline for monitoring new leads.
- Consider ISO or other quality-accreditation processes.
- Make conscious decisions about where to invest your money.

Stage 3: Spreading

Key characteristics

Having successfully navigated your growing business through the 'starting up' and 'forming' stages, it's time to tackle the next stage—spreading.

This is where many businesses find their growth slowing, or even stopping. The key reason is that bringing order to the chaos of the formation stage can inhibit the flexibility and creativity of your business. There's always a trade-off between creativity/innovation and efficiency, and it's easy to get caught on the wrong side of it.

The characteristics of a business at this stage include:

- **Maturing:** By this we mean achieving a level of stability where the rush and hype of the startup phase has passed, and everyone realizes that running a business is very much a job. Growing up means facing the reality of:
  - hiring and firing people
  - being mindful of the positive and negatives of business ownership

- developing a more mature approach to business development and growth.

With several years of business building under your belt, you can now face what would have previously been a crisis with confidence, wisdom and calm. You have a strong base of loyal customers invested in your success who are a great source of the insight needed to drive innovation.

- **Stabilizing:** This term has multiple meanings.

  Financially, it means you've developed strong recurring revenues that provide financial stability and are no longer living 'hand to mouth'.

  Organizationally, it means you've hired managers to build and maintain different functions within your business. You've established an organizational structure that identifies your people and where they fit within the company—both laterally and vertically.

  Culturally, it means your business has achieved its own independent existence beyond the goodwill of the owners, and your employees feel they work for the company, not the owners.

- **Management Layer:** You've acknowledged the need for professional managers, and acted on it. They bring focus and experience, and help create systems, processes and ultimately efficiency.

  It's a key step, both symbolically and practically. Symbolically, it demonstrates your faith in the future of the company by investing in human resources. Practically, it's an acknowledgment that the founding team can't do it all.

  As an SME, hiring people and attracting talent is one of the most crucial and challenging steps towards achieving growth potential. It's also one of the most difficult because you need to get others to believe in the company's vision and potential.

Spreading pressures

Businesses in the spreading stage typically have 30 or more employees. It's a difficult size—too many people for owners to manage effectively, too few to capture the full benefits of a mature structure with business specialists.

Here are the key pressures businesses face at this stage:

- **Diseconomies of scale:** A diseconomy of scale is the opposite of what many people expect from growth—an economy of scale. Diseconomies of scale arise when it costs more to generate each additional dollar of revenue. It happens when you become less efficient as you grow (something we'll look at in more detail later). Suffice to say, if your profit line isn't growing as fast as your revenue line (or at all) it's a warning sign—especially if you aren't consciously investing in your business capability. Which leads to...

- **Increased overheads:** While hiring new people is a necessary and expected part of growing the business, it also results in increased business overheads. (Business overheads can kill businesses because they're not linked to cash flow as costs of sales.) Overheads can also increase at this stage due to:
  - the need to increase business insurances
  - higher occupancy costs on larger premises
  - investment in technology to support the larger workforce and manage customers.

At this stage you must track and manage these increased cost structures through a more mature accounting system that can (at a minimum) provide monthly cash flow forecasts of costs against sales. Businesses often grow their top line at a lower proportional rate than the bottom line, leading to reduced profitability but higher profit.

- **Reduced flexibility:** Another risk is a fixed organizational structure that strangles innovation by hindering the ability to respond quickly and in an unstructured way. People define their abilities by what they do today, rather than thinking like a startup and considering what the world needs tomorrow. It's why many businesses get 'stuck' in this phase, or feel their pace and speed of growth is slowing down. (Smaller businesses can spot gaps in the market and reform people and resources to address them quickly without having to instigate major changes.)

- **Hierarchical decision making:** At this stage you're probably starting to feel the difficulty of having to work through others to get what you want. But unless you want to be a dictator (which isn't a good way to operate), you'll also have to let them form their own decisions. So it's vital that your company has a clear purpose and vision you can communicate to your people so their decisions align with yours. You'll also need to accept that sometimes people will make better decisions, and at other times you'll need to make a 'captain's call'.

What to do

This stage is all about making growth a part of the company's fabric—'baking it in' so to speak. This means being prepared to highlight the tradeoffs between efficiency and creativity.

- **Get external guidance.** Owners often find it useful to get external input on their business. And given that most of them are doing things for the first time, it's a wise move. They may want input on how to:
  - manage the finances of the business
  - establish effective hiring processes
  - develop human resources polices that support retention of quality people.

  That input can come from:
  - formal or informal mentors
  - business groups that offer membership-based networking

- consultants hired to support the business owners with advice and project-based counsel.

One of the benefits of today's contingent workforce is that it's easy to engage high-quality consultants to work in your business on a particular problem or solution for a period of time.

- **Establish a leadership team.** The best way to ensure decisions are aligned with your interests and goals is to create and maintain a tight-knit leadership team—the core group of people you'll operate through. By spending time with them, you can ensure they understand the business goals and leverage their time and abilities to the fullest. But give them space to work and license to be autonomous, because creative and ambitious people rarely thrive in a dictatorship.

- **Review your vision and mission.** You may want to bring in some outsiders to make sure your company vision and mission are realistic, clear, and well communicated. You can also involve your own people by asking them to reflect on the purpose of the company, and their place in helping to achieve it. Incorporate the vision and mission into your induction process so people know them from day one.

- **Review your strategy.** Now's a good time to run a ruler over your business' purpose and determine the essence of what you do and how it should guide your company structure so you can optimally deliver on it.

It's also a good time to consider your first restructure, particularly if the company formed as a result of gradual change, to meet gradually-changing requirements.

Tips for managing growth in the spreading phase

Telltale signs you need to transform during this phase:

- Slowing revenue growth as sales plateau
- Revenue primarily from existing clients rather than new clients
- Indecisiveness in decision making
- Losing focus in the company – trying to do too many things or operate across too many opportunities
- Losing focus on customer needs.

Typical mistakes people make at this stage:

- Losing motivation to keep growing
- Not giving your senior leadership space to contribute and grow
- Becoming too inward-focused and forgetting about the customers
- Trying to do too many things at once, instead of focusing on doing a few things really well
- Becoming set in your ways with how things should be done and what 'best' means.

Stage 4: Corporatization

Key Characteristics

By the time you reach this stage, you're running a fully-fledged business. The irony is that if you set out to run your own small business, the traits you were looking for may well have been lost somewhere along the way.

At this stage, the business should be structured around vertical lines of capability such as:

- employees
- finance
- sales and marketing
- customers and account management
- products
- technology.

You may even have a strategy team to ensure the business is aware of market dynamics and keeping pace with the changes.

In short, you're running your own mini corporation.

- **Hierarchy:** This is the organizational chart that defines reporting relationships throughout the company. A company of this size will almost certainly have managers managing other managers. For example, the head of sales will have a team of sales managers aligned to a particular client industry or grouping, with sales people or account managers reporting to a particular sales manager. While this structure provides benefits such as control and career paths for people, it can also be the genesis of office politics because it creates competition for seniority.

- **Product lifecycle management:** Product lifecycle management is how a product is managed over time, and applies to both physical products and services. A product lifecycle details on the product's introduction and growth, as well as decisions on how to enhance, develop, improve and market it. The original products and services you developed are probably still relevant, but you'll need to develop a process to renew and manage the lifecycle of each one. By this we mean systematically improving your offers through controlled development and upgrades. Product lifecycles ensure your business is aligned to the latest market trends, and provide focus in how you reinvest into the business over time.

- **Looking for secondary opportunities:** As your core product offering matures, and revenue from new and existing clients cools, you need to think about how you can leverage your customer relationships to grow new lines of revenue. This extension growth pathway can create tension between:

- maintaining and supporting your core offering
- being distracted by investing in speculative concepts with uncertain rewards.

But identifying, creating and developing new concepts is a necessary growth strategy at this stage. You should invest our principles of listening and innovating at every level of the company so you know where to look and what to focus on.

- **Doing business in new places:** The other likely growth pathway at this stage is geographic expansion. Going down this pathway may involve developing sales channel partnerships with complimentary businesses, or setting up offices in new areas or countries. In these markets you may be perceived as a new player, and so you need to find ways to establish customer relationships 'cold'. Try networking or going through formal tender search channels.

Corporatization Pressures

At this stage you've pretty much transcended the Small Medium Enterprise moniker, and you'll face new challenges and pressures beyond the scope of this book. Remember our chapter on consciously deciding whether you want to grow? This is where some of the following may come in to play:

- **Loss of purpose:** While conquering the growth curve and achieving sustainable growth and impressive size, you may have lost the very essence of your innovative business. If your original purpose was to disrupt, do things in a new way or be super customer focused, then these motivations may now be redundant. By their very nature, larger businesses are bound to different motivations such as generating profit, supporting employees, and creating and sustaining their market leadership.

You may be the hunted instead of the hunter. Your focus may be short-term instead of long-term. You may even be less risk averse because there's more to lose.

In short, things will have changed. And from a personal perspective, not necessarily for the better.

- **Red tape:** All that time and money spent on developing processes and documenting your offer to drive efficiency and manage risk may turn on you in the form of red tape. Operating in a system that demands recording activity and justifying actions for organizational control inevitably slows things down. But it can also suck the life blood out of a business and increase costs in both time and money. To a degree it's unavoidable at this scale of operation. But be wary of people who prioritize process over client focus and responsiveness.

- **Loss of innovation:** Similarly, the expanding internal focus of your business and the shift towards structure and form can suck the lifeblood out of innovation. Businesses of this size often commission market research to look for answers on what their customers think or where things are going in the market. While this can be a legitimate activity, it can also suggest that your ability to listen and innovate has been strangled by the bureaucracy of a larger company. This is a good time to re-read *Listen, Innovate, Grow*.

- **Loss of people:** A wise person once said, "Never hire someone without expecting they will eventually leave". While it may not be true in practice, it can trigger a useful thought process that ensures you don't rely on individuals to maintain the viability of your businesses.

Earlier in your growth trajectory, losing employees may have triggered feelings of rejection or even personal doubts, depending on their seniority and closeness to the business. As you grow, loss of people becomes something systematic that can bleed you over time. People's motivations for joining your business may be different, and the rewards your business presents aren't the same as those of the smaller business.

The key to managing people attrition is to monitor and understand why people are leaving and where they're going. If they're leaving to join your competitors then all is not well, and you risk losing intellectual property. So it's worth investing in a good exit interview process and strong contractual mechanisms to protect your intellectual property, including non-compete clauses. You can retain your top talent through options and company bonus programs that reward effort, initiative and continued contribution to growth.

What to do

The essence of successful corporatization is realizing the benefits of process and structure to deal with a larger employee base without bureaucracy calcifying your business. But many business fail, and in doing so lose their innovation mojo. Factors that drive successful corporatization include:

- **Developing formal product management lifecycles:** Understand where a particular product sits in its lifecycle, from cash cow to growth engine. This informs decisions on investment so you efficiently invest capital to maximize growth in the short, medium and long term. The Three Stages of Growth model is critical to achieving this.

- **Restructuring your business in mind of key revenue channels:** Over time the business changes, with new customers coming on board and innovation shifting what the company delivers to its clients. Although it's disruptive, restructuring lets you periodically realign your human resources and capability to optimize delivery to your markets and customers.

- **Doubling down on marketing and building your brand to support your extension into new markets:** Once you have the size that generates economies of scale (particularly if you followed the multi-tenanting principle), you'll be able to generate disproportionate profits from each additional customer. This makes investing in marketing and adopting the marketing innovation principles previously outlined even more important.

- **Creating formal quality and risk management techniques:** At a certain size, the need to formalize risk management becomes critical. Adopting quality assurance standards and having an internal focus on quality is an important step to lowering the cost of failure while protecting your brand and corporate reputation.

- **Developing employee benefits programs to attract and lock in talent:** Businesses of this size are in a sweet spot to attract talent with a great mix of growth potential and maturity. (Later in the book we'll examine the importance of your people, and attracting and retaining the best talent.)

Tips to manage growth in the corporatization phase

- Encourage people to work on 'skunk works' projects to cut through red tape
- Place your bets for big winners. Find opportunities with big payoffs and invest in them
- Be prepared to break things to avoid calcification
- Practice management by walking around and keeping your ear to the ground
- Refocus what you do and how you contribute as a leader
- Consider hiring a CEO

Chapter Summary

As we outlined in the previous section, the growth of your company may fundamentally change how your business operates, as well as the demands it places on you and those who work in it. This in turn means that a company that doesn't adapt how it operates as it grows is likely to perform less efficiently.

In short, the ways of doing things that worked just fine for a company with one or two employees and a turnover of several hundred thousand dollars probably won't work for a company with fifty or more people and a turnover of tens of millions of dollars.

Summarizing all the stages we've covered, there are really only two constraints to growth.

1. **Pipeline growth constraint (not generating enough revenue and income to invest in growth strategies):** Growing your pipeline means capturing more opportunities and/or converting those opportunities more successfully into sales to fund further growth. Capturing more opportunities means understanding the 'path to purchase' and converting customers at each level of the pipeline. This includes:

   • increasing awareness among your target audience

   • inducing consideration by identifying your points of difference and clearly differentiating from your competitors

   • inducing purchasing by creating a compelling value proposition including a definition of a return on investment using case studies and testimonials

2. **Operational growth constraint (not transforming your business as you grow to cope with increased revenue and client servicing requirements):** By this we mean how your people, processes and capabilities adapt to the increased demands of company growth. (Think of it as 'scaling up'). This includes:

- production pressures – not keeping up with demand
- customer pressures – not meeting customer needs, which leads to dissatisfaction
- people pressures – not developing your human resources to keep pace in a larger operation
- planning pressures – not developing organizational capabilities that support a forward view on income and profit, allowing proactive investment in the business.

....

Take action now

Review your business to identify constraints.

- Review your business to determine which stage best describes it.
- Identify pressures that exist in the business and list them.
- Review the success factors of the stage your business is at, and think about others that aren't listed.

Mark pipeline growth constraints and take action.

- Create awareness that you're a potential supplier.
- Clearly define your value proposition in a compelling way to generate enquiries.
- Provide prospective customers with channels to purchase.
- Clearly enunciate your value proposition and use case studies to bring it to life in the real world.
- Upsell customers to better products or try cross-selling to increase the depth of your relationship.

Market operational growth constraints and take action.

- Integrate steps to address issues in your business as part of your annual planning cycle (as described earlier in the book).
- Review the pressures in your business, categorize them, and develop actions and strategies to address them through your planning cycle.
- Communicate with your customers and keep them on the journey.

CHAPTER 11

Financials of growth and innovation

Chapter overview

At the simplest level, your business is a cash-generating machine. It takes inputs, runs them through one or more processes to add value, and then sells the output. The gap between the costs of production and revenue from sales is operating income which, if you have a good business, is profitable. You then choose what to do with that income—take it out of the business, or retain it as operating cash or capital investment to fund further growth. Every stage involves decisions about how to raise and spend cash to generate the greatest possible return in the short, medium and long term. A growing business is one where free cash flow is invested back into the business in return for expected increased income and profit.

Cash is the lifeblood of a growing business. If it isn't managed properly and thoughtfully, the business won't achieve its potential. It may even fail. It's that simple.

This book isn't about finance or accounting. But our focus on B2B SME growth warrants a discussion on managing financials in a growth business, because poor financial management will make everything else in this book irrelevant. On the other hand, understanding the implications of growth on money in an SME is a key factor in growth.

In this chapter we will focus on how cash is generated and used in a growing business, and offer practical advice and tips on how to ensure you don't mess it up.

To master financials in a growing B2B SME, you need to understand three key things:

- **How the business generates income**, including how and why this changes as you grow.
- **How the business spends its income**, focusing on overheads and costs of sales that fund current income and capital investments to fund future income.
- **How the business receives income** (i.e. your billing and payments cycle).

The nature of money and innovation

Money funds growth. Without money it's hard to grow, and having money makes growth a lot easier. The paradox is that you need money to grow and growth drives money. So how can you ever get started?

Every business needs starting capital to pay for equipment, office space, salaries and so forth. Most start with some level of funding, whether it's the owner's savings, a loan from a bank or benefactor, or starting capital from an investor. But it's what happens after the starting capital is raised that interests us in this book.

Innovation can continue being funded by outside interests or the bank, and that's a viable way to go about it. However, in this section we'll examine strategies you can use to fund growth within your business. The benefit of doing it this way is you don't lose control of the business, either from repossession by a bank or loss of ownership to outside capital.

This doesn't mean you should never seek outside funding to catalyze or expedite growth when you need to or the opportunity exists. It simply provides a pathway to sustainable, intrinsically-funded growth.

Here are the key ideas and principles we want to focus on:

- For the purpose of this book, money is *potential*. Money gives you choices to do things that otherwise wouldn't exist.

- Innovation costs money in the form of R&D and investment in capability to drive product, service and process innovation.
- Money only has value from an innovation perspective if it isn't tied up in the business and can be used speculatively. The more free cash flow you have, the more you can innovate.
- Any decision on how to invest free cash flow on innovation needs to consider the rate of return in that decision. (This has already been touched upon in McKinsey's *Three Stages of Growth* model.)
- As an owner, taking money out of the business is an opportunity cost because you forego the choice of investing in your business. If there are innovation opportunities that will generate above-normal returns, then it's okay to divert the money to other purposes such as making yourself happy or giving it to someone else making good returns.

Understanding these principles is fundamental to managing your business finances, and how you invest in innovation will help you make good decisions about what you do. These are fairly high-level ideas, so let's start with more basic ideas—how you generate money, how you spend it, and how this will change as your company grows.

How a business generates income in a growth B2B SME

As we outlined in the overview, the process of generating income involves taking inputs, transforming them in some way, and generating outputs. The inputs, processes and outputs can vary, depending on the type of business you're running. For example:

- In a business consultancy, the inputs could be information and consultant hours. The transformation is the distillation and analysis of facts and data into strategic insights. The output is a report and business consulting advice.

- In a trucking company, the output is freight and the movement of goods. The inputs are trucks, planes and trains, as well as the software and people needed to manage the logistics of these movements.
- In a software company, the inputs are developer hours, electricity and IT hardware. The output is a service or product that adds value to another business (e.g. a tool to manage money, time or other resources).

These simple examples illustrate the many ways B2B SMEs can transform inputs into outputs (adding value along the way) to generate profit. **How well you do this** directly translates into how much income you generate, which gives you choices about investing in growth.

The amount of money you can charge for what you do depends on:

- how much value it provides to the clients
- how differentiated you are from your competitors
- how much competition exists in your industry category.

Once a price is set for your goods or services, income is generated based on customers' volume of consumption. The income is then generated by submitting an invoice to the customer that specifies payment terms under a contract of agreement. You receive the income when you're paid.

Each month, depending on sales in preceding months and terms of payment, you'll receive income from your customers. This income can then be:

- used to fund your business in the current month
- set aside for your personal benefit
- invested in the company to generate more future income.

Of course, there are different forms of payment and invoicing that are beyond the scope of this book. But it literally pays to understand how your business does it, and how your own clients and suppliers are paid.

Here's a summary of the types of growth you can expect in income at each stage of development.

Stage	How income grows
Stage I: Starting up Typically 1-10 people	• Foundation customers coming on board • Increasing your share of their spend by offering better value
Stage II: Spreading Typically 10-30 people	• New customer relationships forming through positive word of mouth • Innovation leading to new revenue streams through line extensions and new products/services • Investing in marketing and promotion to drive scaled awareness and consideration in your addressable market (i.e. broadening the funnel and leads to new opportunities to acquire customers) • Increasing prices once the value of your services are established and your brand equity increases
Stage III: Forming Typically 30-100 people	• Expanding geographically • Continuing development of value-added services and product line extensions • Increasing investment in marketing and promotion
Stage IV Corporatizing Typically 100+ people	• Expanding overseas • Gaining efficiency from multi-tenanting products • Developing economies of scale with increasing returns on centralized functions • Developing high-price premiums based on market reputation and premium positioning

How a business spends income in a growth B2B SME

Business costs are classified as either **overheads** or **costs of sales** (also known as **costs of revenue**).

When it comes to managing for growth, these costs are fundamentally different. And knowing the difference between the two is the key to ensuring you're pricing for a profitable growing business.

Overheads: what it costs to run your business

Overheads are the *fixed* costs needed to run your business (salaries, electricity, rent, insurance premiums, etc.). When considering profit, these are amortized or spread across sales revenue.

Overheads are a fixed cost because they need to be paid but aren't linked to sales. Even if you lose sales you still need to pay your overheads, and you can end up losing money. So you need to manage overheads carefully.

As you grow, your overheads will increase. In most cases they'll increase gradually. But they can also grow in large steps, especially when you're hiring.

In the previous section we looked at growth stages, and they're good milestones to consider how overheads will grow in first three stages of growth

Stage	Why overheads grow
Stage I: Starting up Typically from one to ten people	<ul><li>Owners start drawing salaries/distributions from the business</li><li>Software and licensing costs increase</li><li>Insurance costs increase</li><li>Salary costs for customer facing/specialist roles increase</li></ul>

Stage	Why overheads grow
Stage II: Forming Typically ten to 30 people	• Salaries from general manager roles increase • Compliance costs to cover process development increase • Insurance costs continue to increase • Accounting costs increase as operations become more complex • New clients coming on board increase transaction costs • Increased spend on marketing and sales acquisition
Stage III: Spreading Typically 30 to 100 people	• Strategic investment in the business to expand offering • General overheads continue to increase in line with growth –rent, P&E, insurances, wages, etc. • Increased spending on marketing and sales acquisition
Stage IV Corporatizing Typically 100 +	• More of the above but on a bigger scale • Insourcing of outsourced function such as marketing, legal and strategy • Introducing new layers of management

Costs of sales: what it costs to generate income

Costs of sales are the variable costs linked to each unit of a sale, whether it's a nut, a bolt, an item delivered, a property sold, a loan financed, a building plumbed or a billed project hour. As your sales vary, the cost of sales go up and down.

Costs of sales hold back your profitability unless you innovate to gain scale (i.e. increase sales disproportionately to costs). If your costs of sales grow in line your with revenue, your business won't scale up efficiently and your revenue will grow more than your overall profit.

The costs of sales are external costs. They're what you pay suppliers to produce what you sell to customers. Money goes out the door to fund more money coming in the door.

When you report your financial results, your costs of sales are taken from revenue to calculate your **gross margin**. Gross margin is the profit you make before factoring in:

- overheads
- revenue from non-core business activities
- interest
- tax.

As you grow, you can start generating additional profit by lowering your costs of sales. You could do this by:

- renegotiating your contracts with your suppliers to reflect the greater volume you're buying
- insourcing your costs of sales and convert them to (lower) cost per unit sales overheads
- trying to eliminate them altogether by changing how you produce your product or service, either with technology or through innovation.

Instead of thinking of your suppliers as a cost of sale, think of them as a partner. Just as you want your loyal clients to think of *you* as a partner by working closely together and sharing the rewards of a mutual relationship, we suggest doing the same with your suppliers by:

- sharing value with them
- communicating opportunities
- working with them collaboratively.

While your ultimate aim may be to reduce how much you spend with them to increase profit, pressuring them into lowering their prices by getting lots of potential suppliers to quote is a false economy. Treating supplier relationships as a transaction rather than as a partnership will ultimately hold your business back from generating cost savings and innovating. (It's also a hypocritical way to run your growth business.)

The strategy of reducing costs of sales by bringing them in-house and making them overheads needs to be carefully considered and financially modelled. One way is by hiring someone internally to do the work you currently contract out to a consultant. The main reason for doing this is to increase profitability—you can spread the overhead across all your sales, resulting in a lower cost per unit of revenue. It also gives you more control over your supply chain in terms of timing and quality.

But outsourcing has its own appeals, the main one being you won't incur any cost unless you sell something. This means you can still maintain your profit during quiet periods. There's also the 'stick to your knitting' argument that you should let the expert give you the best possible input to your own product process.

Ultimately it boils down to whoever can produce the business input at the required quality for the lowest unit price.

How you engage with your suppliers and spend your money is critical to a growth business because:

- insourcing versus outsourcing is a natural lever that balances risk with profit
- what you do yourself and what you get others to do will determine what you focus on, and hence where you want to play
- the amount of free cash flow in your business gives you choices about where to invest for innovation.

Lack of cash flow can kill your business

Everyone knows this one. It's repeated ad nauseum in business books and courses. But saying it once more won't hurt.

Lack of cash flow can kill your business.

Here's what you can do to ensure you don't run out of money.

- Run a three-month float. Keep the money in a safe place where you won't be tempted to dive into it (e.g. a term deposit or specific holding account).

- Spend a few hours every month reviewing your forecast. You should step through what revenue is expected, what costs are expected, and forecast your net cash position at 30 days (if not 60 days) horizon.

- Be aware of your trade debtors, and categorize outstanding payments in 30-day, 60-day and 90-day brackets. Understand how (and when) specific customers pay, and get to know their accounts payable people so you can follow up when necessary. Don't be afraid to follow up at the 60-day mark, or even earlier. A good customer will understand that as a small business, you have specific payment terms that aren't as lenient as large corporates.

- When forecasting, be conservative. Don't assume customers will pay on time (they generally don't).

- Manage your costs of sales by telling your suppliers they'll get paid when you get paid. A good supplier will accept this if you give them:

  - clarity regarding your payment cycle
  - notice as to where payments stand.

This strategy is one of the most important and effective steps you can take to ensure you don't run out of cash.

Be aware of your annual profit cycle, particularly the 'lumpy' months. For example, many customers accrue payments at the end of the financial year to help manage their budget and minimize their tax. This means your revenue can surge at the end of the financial year, and then drop off the following month.

Depending on how taxes work in your country or jurisdiction, certain months may be expensive than others. Make sure you've made provisions to cover these higher-than-normal costs.

Billing and payment cycles

The third key aspect to managing your financials is the billing and payment cycle.

Sales and payment are not the same thing. You record sales, but then you need to collect them (as a credit to your account) at a later point—often after your product or service has been produced or delivered. It happens this way whether you run an accrual or cash accounting system.

This is one of the key differences between B2B and B2C. B2B payments are often made in arrears by invoicing or running accounts on quite generous terms (e.g. 30 to 60 days). And it can cause problems, particularly for a growing business that pays its people every month without fail.

You can also make it work the other way with your suppliers (i.e. you can string them out to maintain cash flow). But don't string out payments to your employees unless you want to lose them all and trash your reputation as both a business and an employer.

A key reason businesses fail is they don't understand this timing disparity. Managing your financials in a growing business means:

- understanding your monthly fixed cost structure
- understanding what your costs of sales are per transaction

- understanding how much cash you have in the bank at any given time
- being able to forecast your future revenue and future costs
- making contingencies for known costs against revenue
- maintaining a 'float' – this is accessible cash to pay bills that has no committed spend.

Each month your business will have money going out and money coming in. The challenge is to forecast your income for that month against costs you expect to come in that month.

You also need to know how much cash you will have in the bank. This is the float, and it's what lets you sleep at night.

The float is the number of months of 'coverage' you have if you lost all your clients overnight. A good rule of thumb is to have a 3-month float, which means that if you didn't earn any revenue for three months your business would still be able to cover its costs.

In a growth business where cash is consumed by growing, having a strong float is critical. You may hear that growing a business means profit is secondary. While it may be true for capitalized businesses that want to gain market leadership as quickly as possible, is doesn't need to be like that. You can sustainably fund growth through client led-innovation.

Going back to our principles of finance and innovation, your float isn't just your layer of financial protection. It's also your 'pool of potential innovation'. It's your own inbuilt kickstarter that gives you choice on how and where to invest. Learn how much is in it, how quickly it gets replenished and from where. Once you find out, you'll be in a position to know how to use it.

Invoicing should never be overlooked when things get busy

- Invoice early and invoice often.
- Negotiate the most favorable payment terms (ideally 30 days or less).
- Ensure your accounts payable payment terms are aligned with your customer payment terms.
- Track your invoices on days outstanding – 30, 60, 90+ days.
- Have a process to follow up with customers when invoices are late, and don't be afraid to do so.
- Never assume you'll be paid on time in your cash forecasts.
- Be wary of first-time clients, particularly other small businesses. Ensure you have special payment terms in such cases (e.g. a proportion that must be paid up front).

How costs and overheads grow as you grow

As we said earlier, a key tenet of growing your business is that it costs money to grow. This implies that you need to make provisions for investing in your business outside of the normal day-to-day expenditure patterns your business should account for. The hard part is you don't always know where the costs will arise, or their magnitude.

Not all of your investments will pay off. You may have hired the wrong people, invested in technology that was superseded, or simply spend your money in the wrong way. It's the nature of the game.

The trick is to make as few mistakes as possible and get it right most of the time. Being customer-led gives you important guidance on how and where to spend money on the business by aligning it to a demonstrated customer need you can meet with a product or service—not just for one customer, but for many.

Here are some of the costs you should expect to grow in a healthy and innovative B2B SME.

- **Marketing costs:** This is all about investing in your brand, promotions, communications, developing collateral and content to distribute through social media. You can do this up to a point by engaging external agencies. But they tend to charge hefty fees for creative work with an unproven return on investment. Being marketers themselves, expect them to try to upsell you on everything. Stick to the basic premise that effective marketing:

    - identifies a need
    - communicates the benefits of the product
    - differentiates you from your competitors.

    Also consider implementing some of the cost-effective marketing innovation approaches we outlined earlier in this book, such as advocacy marketing.

- **Hiring new people:** In our experience, it takes a new person at least six months to become productive in their job. This means hiring people increases your overheads without driving an increase in productivity (at least not initially). One beneficial trend we've seen in recent years is the rise of contract workers. These days you can easily parachute in a ready-to-go, high-capability consultant to take on a specific task or build capability ready for someone less experienced to pick up and grow. This approach can be particularly useful for strategic consulting, marketing, and developing new capability in the business.

- **Insurance:** Business insurance, particularly professional indemnity and public liability, is generally assessed on your annual turnover and the number of employees you have. This means insurance costs will grow as your business grows and your risks increase.

Consider whether a particular contract requires unusually high coverage or terms. This can increase your insurance costs dramatically, and will need to be factored in when costing a particular opportunity or project.

- **IT costs:** If you don't watch them carefully, your IT costs can grow exponentially. Their growth is tied to needing to invest in new IT support capability while also maintaining existing capability and integrating with it. You should consider buying off-the-shelf solutions and customizing them rather than hiring developers to create bespoke solutions. As developer tools get better and better, bespoke solutions are certainly an option. However, be wary of the ongoing maintenance costs needed to keep up with the latest technology.

  Upgrading IT hardware such as employee computers and phones can also cost a small fortune. But the payoff is an increase in productivity and general work satisfaction.

- **Subscriptions:** Owners or specialists in a good 'listening' business will spend time reading industry magazines, newsletters and trade publications. While the subscription costs can quickly mount up, they should be seen as a key investment for your business.

- **Training:** A multiplier cost of having more people is they need to be trained. Depending on your industry, training costs can be expensive, particularly if you need to maintain professional development as part of professional accreditation. However, high-quality content is often available from online training providers at low cost, or even free. A good way to manage your training budget is to allocate a specific budget for each employee, which they can manage autonomously. (You can assess how they're using their training budget as part of the employee review cycle.)

- **Travel:** If your business is expanding geographically, you should expect to spend more on travel. An obvious solution is to charge travel costs back to your clients where possible by making it an explicit item in your contract or statement of work.

While teleconferencing can largely mitigate travel costs, never underestimate the benefits of regular face-to-face meetings with your most valued clients.

- **Rent:** A sure sign you're doing well in your business is running out of room for your new employees or equipment. But while this is exciting is can also be potentially expensive, especially if you're leasing your premises on a term contract. Breaking a contract can be expensive and risky, and renting more space means spending more money on your lease.

  While rent can be expensive, consider it a worthwhile investment in its own right. Many studies have shown that people's productivity is strongly related to their work environment. Working out of a garage may seem 'cool', but the poor aesthetics, lack of space and terrible ergonomics can quickly become an issue. A nice work environment in a desirable location increases your ability to become an employer of choice and attract high-quality talent.

- **Plants and equipment:** For manufacturing companies, transport companies, retailers and other businesses with physical inventory, increasing demands means buying plant and equipment to support customer demands. (Depreciating and managing assets is beyond the scope of this book, but you should know that purchasing or even leasing new equipment can tie up capital.)

- **Inventory costs:** As a general rule, larger retailing and manufacturing companies must buy and hold more inventory. As a growing company, this can be particularly challenging. You need to manage forward orders while balancing availability and delivery times with carrying excess non-earning inventory. (The more inventory you carry, the lower your return on capital.)

- **Product development:** Software development and integration needed for process automation involves spending money on developers, either on contract or outsourced. Money spent on development can quickly mount up, and it pays to consider the merits of buying off-the-shelf software that meets your needs before committing to developing solutions in-house.

- **Intellectual Property (IP) Costs:** If you're creating new products or services, you may want to protect them with copyrights and trademarks.

  Copyright protects your invention from being copied by others. While this sounds like a sensible step to take, it's an expensive and risky business that takes years to proceed and has an uncertain outcome. You should apply for copyright in every country you trade in (or intend to trade in), which means your costs can quickly multiply.

  Trademarking is protecting a name, device or other symbol to prevent others using it. This helps you maintain distinctiveness, and ensures consumers know your product. The trademarking process varies from country to country, but typically it's less expensive and less time-consuming than copyrighting.

At some point you may want to borrow money or take on an investor who can provide cash to fund your growth. Debt funding and raising capital is beyond the scope of our book, but here are a few brief points:

- The main reason for doing this is when you can't reach your growth objectives with the funding you generate intrinsically from your business. Another reason for doing it is to tap into an investor network for advice or access to new clients through investor networks. But if you choose to go down this route, be very clear about your funding objectives. Don't do it because it sounds cool, or because you think you can raise big dollars.

- Getting funding is distracting. You spend a lot of time talking to people about your business and what you do, which means you're effectively losing IP even when you sign a non-disclosure agreement. Even though preparing investor packs does get you thinking about your business, it's still taking you away from working in your business.

  Worst of all, it may never end. Once you get funded you'll probably end up going through multiple rounds of funding, which means you'll be spending a lot of time telling others what you're doing and justifying your choices. This can be stressful and unrewarding.

- Borrowing from a bank costs money in the form of interest. Unless you can use the money to generate more revenue than the interest costs, you're going backwards. But if you can use the money to fund growth beyond these costs then by all means borrow it.

  Borrowing also creates risk. (It's why you have to pay to use other people's money.) More risk usually means more stress. If you're having a period of poor cash flow the banks will still expect to be paid. If you default they can call in creditors, which will probably be the death knell for your business.

The virtuous circle of client-funded innovation

One of the benefits of the LIG framework is it provides a way for your customers to sustainably fund your growth. This virtuous circle of client-funded innovation and product development means you don't have to borrow or take outside funds to invest in your product **providing your clients fund your growth in a way that benefits them too.**

The basic premise of this virtuous circle, uniquely suited to B2B SMEs and the LIG framework, can be summarized as follows:

1. You listen to your customers for points of frustration, opportunity, desire, and need (as outlined in the Listen chapters of this book).

2. You invest in innovation that saves your client money or generates incremental value.

3. You develop your innovation in such a way that it can be offered to other clients at low marginal cost (the multi-tenanting principle).

4. You don't charge your client for developing the underlying innovation. Instead you charge them for the end product or service that arises *from* the innovation.

5. You make this arrangement transparent and sign a non-compete agreement to retain your client's contribution to developing the IP. You unambiguously own and retain the IP.

6. You actively cross-sell the innovation to other clients, and use it to enhance the appeal of your business to the market.

This is the virtuous circle the LIG framework unlocks for your business. It does it at no cost to you, in a way *everyone* benefits from – you, your direct client and your broader clientele.

Sales and financial management disciplines for client-led innovation

Achieving growth through the virtuous circle of client-led innovation involves the following financial disciplines.

Identify the Change Agents and treat them well

The Change Agents we talked about in Chapter 3 usually love being involved in projects that develop new capabilities. And chances are they'll be happy to fund projects that innovate to support their internal goals. They also tend to move around a lot, and will probably take you with them as they move around different companies driving change and mixing things up.

Change Agents love being looked after, having their ideas bought to life, and creating new capabilities for their employers. So if you treat them well, and help them achieve their goals, they can become your best salespeople.

Remove the 'owned IP' clause

Corporate sourcing people often try to make you sign an *owned IP* clause, which basically says any innovation or invention that comes from you delivering your services to the client become *their* property, not yours. This is clearly overreach, and needs to be removed from the contract. The contract must state (directly or indirectly) that the client is paying for delivery of the service—not the product itself. In other words, any innovation you create remains yours. They are only paying for the benefits it provides.

Negotiate hard, and don't roll over.

Charge for the outcome, not the innovation

Make it clear you're charging for the end benefit, not the innovation. In other words, you'll be funding the innovation that drives the output. But you won't be invoicing for anything until the innovation is delivered. This is critical, and must be reflected in the customer contract and all business communications.

Be upfront about it. Embed your proactive stance on customer-led innovation as an overt part of your offer. A great way to do this is to add a line item to your invoice stating the deliverable is the output. If need be, explain that the cost of the innovation is subsidized and not fully costed back to the client.

In essence, they're paying to prioritize the development by pushing it further up your product roadmap. And you *must* make it clear from day one that's exactly what the client is buying.

If possible, treat the deliverable as a service, in order to create a recurrent revenue stream

Recurrent revenue is the financial engine that drives innovation. It's the river that replenishes your pool of capital and gives you choices about where to innovate. If you don't have recurrent revenue, you won't be able to forward plan for your business. Recurrent revenue has a premium in net present value because it's secure and can be counted on.

Even if you have to sacrifice some revenue and profit in the short-term, you're generally much better off creating a long-term source of recurrent revenue to finance your growth. It's stable and arrives regularly, which means you can rely on it to invest in other aspects of your business.

Avoid creating overheads

In every aspect of the product, service or process innovation you create, avoid creating baked-in costs and time-cost overheads. Automate everything as much as possible so each additional sale of the innovation generates maximum profit without needing to increase your overheads or costs of sales. Use technology as much as possible to avoid manual processes and bottlenecks in processes that can undermine the economies of scale that arise from customer-led innovation.

Cross-sell developed IP

Businesses often start with a bunch of great clients 'brought over' by founders who had a previously-formed relationship from another business. Try to stretch your relationships to request case studies and referrals. It's very difficult for large businesses to establish a supplier relationship with an SME with no track record.

Client advocacy is also an effective way to demonstrate the need for your innovation. It shows that *all* of your clients will benefit from your innovation by being in a 'club' where time spent collaborating with you will be repaid by providing innovation led by other non-competing clients. Your business will become the 'hub' of an innovation wheel, with each client being a 'spoke'.

Non-compete strategy

The cost of acquiring business can be lowered by looking for deep relationships rather than lots of clients. Deep customer relationships are more enduring, have lower transaction costs, and drive your company to innovate.

Non-compete strategies have an opportunity cost in the form of foregone opportunities. But if your client thinks their ideas are being shared with competitors, the whole concept of customer-led innovation breaks down. If you're ethical, and do the right thing by your clients, you can't go wrong.

Risks to customer-led innovation financing your retained IP

Here are the main areas to be careful of when developing your customer-led growth strategy.

Not placing boundaries around what you can do

In a close and trusting business relationship, your customer may see you as the 'go-to' company for problem solving. As the saying goes *'if you want to get something done, give it to the busiest person in your team'.* Unfortunately, if you don't learn to say 'no', you'll end up working on all kinds of projects and lose focus.

Knowing where to innovate also means learning to say 'no', because focus is the key to success.

Underestimating the cost and complexity of innovation

It's easy to get caught up in the excitement of a new idea. However, you need to spend time upfront to assess the complexity of the project and the time and capital investment you'll need to make it work. Underestimating leads to projects that can drag you under, particularly when the financial structure of customer-led innovation projects is to frontload the cost and recover the revenue over a long period. Danger signs include:

- a vague brief or specification
- multiple interdependencies in your project plan
- the need to hire new people or take on new skills or technology to develop the capability.

These will all increase your cost base and limit the economies of scale benefits from the innovation.

Not being discerning on what to offer

Even if the assignment is something in your sphere of activity, and there's an opportunity to co-create with your customer in product, service or process innovation, there's a risk it could have limited relevance to other clients. In this scenario you'll almost certainly under-recover on your front-end investment.

Not being clear on IP ownership

We can't emphasize this enough. If you don't make this clear, you could be accused of stealing IP from your client and end up in court.

In summary, the customer-led innovation mindset is the engine that can financially power your growth. Don't be afraid to trade short-term revenue opportunities for long-term benefits to your business.

Process innovation unlocks the Virtuous Double Loop Strategy

In the 1990s, Woolworths created what CEO Roger Corbett called the Virtuous Double Loop Strategy[42]. Simply put, he invested in his supply chain to deliver efficiencies and save costs. The savings were passed on to consumers in the form of reduced grocery prices, which resulted in double-digit growth from 2000–2009.

This Virtuous Double Loop Strategy can also be applied to your B2B SME business, particularly with process innovation.

Investing in **process innovation** should generate efficiencies, which will in turn generate cost savings that can be either retained in the business to increase profit or passed back to your customers to increase the value of your offer. The choice is yours.

Here are some thoughts on this financial decision.

- To determine savings you need to be able to quantify savings, which isn't always easy. Make sure you track your investment in the cost of process innovation initiatives, even if they're all internal. Your investment in the innovation needs to be recovered somewhere too.

- Savings don't need to be passed on as lower costs. They can also be passed on as more competitive pricing on future submissions for other work (i.e. the efficiency from innovation cross-subsidizes your service provision). They could even be used to increase resourcing and service levels for your client.

- If you decide to retain the value to increase profitability, the profits can be reinvested in the business as further innovation. In this sense, retaining the value from your process innovation gives you more choice on how and where to innovate later.

The Virtuous Double Loop Strategy is a key financial enabler for success, and should be part of your planning for any process innovation.

The importance of scaling up your financial management

Not all business managers are good at finances, just as not all finance people are good at growing businesses. Sometimes the two disciplines are at odds, and that's okay. It can be good to have tension between those who want to reduce spending and avoid risk, and those who want to grow and take risks.

The best advice we can give is to get someone to focus on the money. Make sure it's someone that you trust, and who knows what they're doing. It can be a bookkeeper, an accountant or (eventually) your business' finance or accounting person. They'll keep you from making rookie mistakes that can undo all your hard work.

You also need to understand the cost base of your business and ensure you're growing sustainably and in a healthy way. A key argument to support growth is economies of scale. The idea is that larger companies can spread higher revenues across a lower production cost base, leading to more favorable 'economies' and therefore more profit. However, it assumes the processes a business uses to produce outputs will scale up. That is, they have no or diminished marginal costs and additional revenue is inherently more profitable.

A less well-known concept is **diseconomies of scale**. This time the business becomes less profitable as it grows because the production processes become less efficient and marginal costs of production increase with revenue.

This is common for growing businesses of a certain size, typically between 20 and 50 employees. Why? There are two main reasons:

1. **Step increases in business overheads:** When the business is in the 'spreading' stage, it's hiring more people and rapidly increasing other overheads that aren't directly tied to revenue. Initially the costs of these additional overheads is disproportionately higher than the revenue base.

   For example, a business hires a general manager on a $150,000 wage to help it stay in control. This person's wages need to be recovered from new revenue. However, new revenue won't be earned for some time, and so profit decreases.

2. **Increasing demand and revenue creates inefficiencies:** The processes designed and created to generate income from a smaller business don't always scale up well, which means the business becomes less efficient the more it grows.

   For example, a company with a machine that produces packaging may find it breaks down when it's run at peak rates over long period, leading to loss of revenue and angry clients.

   Another example is when one area of the business increases output to the point where another area can't cope, leading to waste and inefficiency.

Being aware of the potential for diseconomies of scale is the first step to minimizing or even avoiding them altogether. Here's what you can do to avoid falling into the trap.

- **Watch your financial numbers closely** and always focus on two key ratios in your business:

  1. The percentage of revenue comprised of cost of sales

2. The percentage of revenue that is being consumed by business overheads.

Together, they give you the simplest view of profitability.

Be particularly attuned to costs of sales or overheads growing disproportionately to revenue growth. Monitor it, and if you see decreases in profit over time, find out why.

- **View your company using the input > process > output lens,** and understand what each person, machine or asset does in that process. Identifying wastage throughout the system from non-productive people and assets. Also look for how production flows through the system, and identify any bottlenecks causing wastage. When you invest in new capacity, make sure the areas of the business affected by the change (sales, marketing, finance, etc.) are ready for it.

- **Whenever you make an investment in the business** (whether it be personnel or new equipment), make sure you understand what the return on that investment will be, and why.

Of course, not all investments are directly involved in production. For example, you could hire a strategy manager whose job is to help you chart the course of the company's direction. But even in this role (or any other role at managerial level) you should expect a payoff in the form of a better business that attracts more clients and makes more money.

Never lose this discipline.

Chapter summary

In this chapter we looked at how growth influences finances, and how financial control is a key factor in successfully managing your business.

You should think of your business as an input > process > output system that creates value for you and your clients. Growing a business costs money, and it may decrease profitability in the short term. Client-led innovation means you can help your customers fund your innovation, and then offer the innovation to the market where there's no competitive relationship. Managing finances sustainably means:

- understanding what costs are growing as your business grows
- invoicing regularly
- tracking invoices
- ensuring you have enough retained earnings for any short-term crisis that may eventuate.

In summary, different startup situations of businesses dictate specific funding arrangements. While some startups are capital-funded with outside investors, most businesses start their life from the hip pockets of their founders and don't rely on capital investment to grow. Some businesses borrow to fund expansion.

In both cases, most business owners recognize the need to not lose money. The challenge is to balance the costs of growth with the pace of growth. Any profit you make can be invested into your business to drive innovation, which will lead to faster growth. But every dollar you take out of the business has an opportunity cost of investment in growth foregone.

Still, if you're not prepared to scale up then the return on your investment will be lower than it should be.

Take action now

1. Review your accounts from previous financial years to understand the mix of overheads and costs of sales. Look at how it's changed as the business has grown. Has it remained the same, or changed over time?

2. Understand how your profit has changed over time. Has it increased or decreased? If it has decreased, is it due to structural (locked in) changes in your cost structure, or is it related to growth factors?

3. Identify whether your forward revenue and revenue annuities are sufficiently stable to convert costs of sales into overheads at a lower marginal cost.

4. Review your terms of payment to determine if you can negotiate more favorable terms.

5. Review your customer contracts to determine whether you've retained intellectual capital in your co-innovation initiatives, or if there's a 'retain IP' clause that could create risk for you. Create a template that specifies you retain any developed IP.

CHAPTER 12

Your people, growth and innovation

Chapter Overview

Change by its very nature can be disconcerting for some people. The growth of a business places demands on the people who run it, operate it and work in it. How you manage its impact on your people is as important as any other factor to your success.

This chapter looks at how a good B2B SME growth manager can deal with the many people issues that arise from rapid growth, and develop an organization with the right people and behaviors for growth. You'll learn how your team will be key contributors to your success, and how without proper management they could be a significant handbrake to your ambitions.

We'll begin by looking at the three pillars of organizational growth:

- Leadership
- Company culture
- Capability.

Once we've examined these pillars, we'll consider the change elements that occur in your company as it grows, and how these changes affect each of the three pillars.

The change elements we'll examine are:

Organizational change elements affected by growth:

- Work environment
- Organizational structure
- Job role needs
- Job support functions

People change elements affected by growth:

- New people join the company
- People leave the company
- People who remain change

After reading this chapter, you'll understand why people are the key factors in successful growth. You'll also know how to manage the changes that affect them to ensure a positive growth experience that leads to increases in productivity, retention and discretionary effort.

Growth pillar 1: Leadership

What is leadership?

While leadership means different things to different people and the meaning can change over time, being a leader in your B2B SME essentially means embodying the spirit of your company and its growth ambitions. You need to be the person people turn to when the path is uncertain and they need to find direction and seek advice. And like it or not, the way you do things sets the standard for how others do things.

The burden of leadership means you must make the big decisions about the course set and how to get to the company goals. You earn your position by making the hard calls and supporting others when things are at their toughest.

A growth leader doesn't calls all the shots, or go around telling people what to do. They never take the easy option. Instead they think ahead to consider how different scenarios may play out and, if necessary, make difficult short-term decisions that support long-term success.

A true growth leader is successful because they create a high-performing team that is greater than the individuals who comprise it. They trust the people around them and listen to what they have to say. But they're not afraid to be the one who makes the decision.

Being a leader in a B2B SME puts certain demands on your leadership. You're not running a company of thousands of people, or even hundreds of people. So in many ways leadership is a more intimate experience, and you can exert influence directly throughout your company.

Traits of successful B2B SME growth leaders

Many words have been written on leadership, and it can mean different things to different people. As a founder of the business you may not have 'signed up' to be a leader, but those who work for you will expect you to demonstrate leadership traits.

But what are these traits?

Based on interviews with leaders, and our research on successful start-ups, here are the common factors we identified among leaders in high-growth B2B SME firms.

1. Visible and approachable

The CEO of a Fortune 500 company can 'hide' in their corner office and deal with their employees, leadership team, HR Managers and the outside world through a corporate communications team.

But you don't have that luxury.

A good B2B SME growth leader knows everyone by name and makes time to walk the floor and be a visible presence in the company. Everyone can take pride in and feel the safety of your relationship with them.

Approachability means everyone in your company feels comfortable approaching you with ideas, concerns, or just to say hello. Having everyone feel a sense of familiarity and a positive personal relationship with you goes a long way to inspiring them.

It's also important to remember that great leaders are often seen as being the best at what they do. They're people who backed their skill and knowledge enough to start their own company, confident their skills would lead to success. As their company grew, the people they bought on board were strongly motivated by the belief that their founders were 'visionary' and 'thought leaders' – the sort of people you want to be around as your career develops so you can learn by osmosis and observation.

2. Sales-driven

Selling, and representing your company to other business people, is intrinsic to success. Along with the big pitch, you need to be able to develop strong customer relationships, smooth things over, and deal with things when they go wrong.

In a study published by McKinsey, two key leadership factors most strongly oriented with growth were **market insight** and **customer impact**, where customer impact is defined as the capacity to understand customers' evolving needs[43]. While not all company founders and leaders are natural salespeople, believing in your product and being able to explain its benefits and value to clients goes a long way to creating and closing opportunities.

3. Strong technical understanding

B2B companies generally need a strong technical understanding of how things work in the business, spanning all activities that occur. You need enough knowledge to 'talk shop' with the people who work for you so you can help them continuously reappraise and get better at what they do. You also need to ensure they direct their creativity and energy in alignment with the company vision.

In short, the growth leader catalyzes the skills of others, linking disparate expertise into a coherent picture. Of course, you need to avoid potential traps such as getting caught in the minutiae and telling people how do to their jobs.

The skill is being able to jump into technical conversations and meaningfully contribute by keeping your people focused on being **customer-centric** and aligned to the **company strategy**. If you listen and contribute with these two thoughts in mind, you really can't go wrong.

4. Inspires through actions

Leading by example is something all growth leaders do well. They're willing to do long hours and 'punch through walls' to reach their goals. When people in the business see the owners going the extra mile, it inspires them to go above and beyond and contribute to the success of the organization.

But when people see their leader always taking the easy options, avoiding hard conversations and generally lacking 'spine', they can quickly lose confidence.

It takes a certain brashness to start your own business and take on the risks that follow. Not just the personal risks, but also accepting responsibility for the wellbeing and welfare of people who choose to follow the company and join. Not everyone can take that initial bet and 'double down' so to speak. Deciding to take hard-earned capital and reinvest it in speculative innovation and growth takes courage. This is why it's one of the key traits that drives loyalty.

5. Self-belief

Successful leaders believe in themselves and what they're doing. Despite setbacks and times of uncertainty, they can galvanize their people with confidence that the ship is steady and the course is true even in the most severe storms. While it's sometimes confused with arrogance, belief is really about self-confidence and being self-contained. Strong leaders don't need positive affirmation from others to believe their direction and choices are worthwhile. A leader who inspires belief is a leader with a strong culture and a committed team who will stick around and dig deep when the going gets tough.

"The biggest challenges in the early stages for any business with growth, particularly when you're taking on established businesses, are getting people to believe in your business, getting people to trust you, and getting them to step away from businesses that are established, have good reputations, and more financially secure."
— *Mark Heron, partner at Connective.*

6. Integrity

In our B2B SME consulting work over the years, great leaders have repeatedly identified the importance of demonstrating integrity—doing as you say, choosing the right way instead of the easy way, and staying true to your ethos and ideas. It also means speaking plainly, and not embellishing facts or avoiding negative feedback.

Integrity justifies the faith of employees in the leader, and removes uncertainty and doubt during the hard times that inevitably arise. When leaders sacrifice integrity for short-term gain or to avoid pain, the company culture is put at risk. Seeing a lack of integrity from founders effectively gives employees permission to operate without integrity themselves. As the saying goes, 'a fish rots from the head'.

7. Nurture talent and grow their people

In great workplaces, people have space to grow and develop. It's tempting to hire people to do what you want them to do, but it doesn't really demonstrate growth leadership.

Effective growth leadership means conveying a clear definition of success (both individually and organizationally) to everyone in your team, and then giving them 'space' to grow their ideas and company capability to support this success.

It's that simple.

By giving people this space, you encourage them to do better. You set them challenges that benefit the company as a whole, and give them the opportunity to contribute meaningfully on the growth journey.

8. Communicate effectively

A key to success in a growing business is acknowledging the need to sell, explain and communicate the company direction and momentum to the people in the business. The role of the growth manager is to be sensitive to the fact that change (particularly sustained change) can be distressing for many people, and that the need for confidence in leadership is heightened compared to a static business.

Stage	What leadership means
Stage I: Starting up Typically 1-10 people	• Taking the pain – working hard and setting the pace • Rolling up the sleeves and getting things done • Spotting trends and jumping on them before others • Being there for clients whenever they're needed
Stage II: Forming Typically 10-30 people	• Stepping back, creating space for others to step in • Remaining calm when things don't work • Developing capabilities of their people • Creating a strong company culture by example
Stage III and IV: Spreading / Corporatization Typically 30+ people	• Delegating to the new management layer • Showing thought leadership • Becoming a leader in their industry • Providing direction and strategic vision

Growth pillar 2: Company culture

What is company culture?

Company culture is the unique personality of a company. It's the group dynamic that emerges from placing people together to make decisions every day about how to work with others and deliver on their own role and objectives.

Culture stems from the founder, as well as the sum of interactions that create a 'vibe' about how things are done in your company.

Company culture can be strong or weak, positive or negative. It can manifest itself in:

- the quality of interpersonal relationships between employees and how they interact
- how clients and suppliers are treated
- levels of effort
- how people share and receive ideas.

Nothing is more important to the success of your company than its culture. It must be aligned to support the success factors we've outlined in this book – listening, innovating and growing.

- **A strong company culture** is one where the rules (written or unwritten) about how to approach things are highly normative—people feel compelled to do things in the same way to align with how others do them.

  A positive company culture is a powerful force for good that can drive people to achieve and work together effectively as a team. But when good companies go bad, 'toxic' cultures can arise, characterized by people being:

- set in their ways
- defensive of change and possessive of their power base
- jealous of the power of others.

This is also known as 'office politics'.

- **A weak company culture** is one where:

  - there are no clear principles on how things are done
  - pretty much anything goes
  - people don't feel any boundaries or constraints about how they behave as individuals within the group.

A company with a weak culture excessively looks to the leader to make all the decisions. Individuals come to work and do just enough to fulfill their job descriptions. Clearly you don't want a weak organizational culture.

To harness your people as part of your engine of growth, you need to develop a strong company culture that's geared towards growth.

Traits of company culture in a successful growth B2B SME

1. Balanced team and individual focus to accept failure as the recipe for success

Cultures in small organizations differ fundamentally to those in large organizations. There should be less politics and greater team cohesion. Because everyone knows everyone else, collective trust and cohesion behind company goals should be stronger.

But there's always the potential for weak culture to undermine a small organization, particularly one where people are paramount. A helpful way to conceptualize culture is by using two spectrums:

1. outcomes (success or failure)
2. individual versus group dynamic.

2. Healthy growth culture matrix

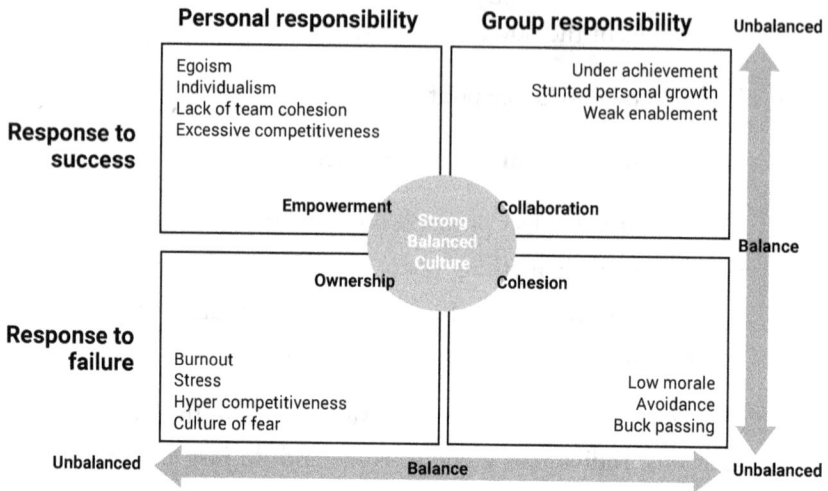

This approach to thinking about your growth culture acknowledges the need for balance in group versus individual responsibility in every situation—good or bad.

A strong company culture is one where the balance is right. People aren't afraid to take personal responsibility for things not going to plan, but not to the extent where they feel the punishing weight of fear of failure that stifles creativity and innovation—critical to growth.

They should also feel they have a critical role to play in their own success. They should be proud of their achievements, while acknowledging their success is only possible through the group efforts of their colleagues in the organization.

On the contrary, a weak or unbalanced culture is one where individuals claim ownership of success and assign failure to others. They blame their inability to achieve their goals on the organization instead of themselves for not taking ownership of their personal growth. In this type of culture, individuals can do a lot of damage by starving others of confidence and displaying egotistical behavior. If you see people acting in this way in your company, remove them—quickly.

3. Motivated by purpose

People who come to work with purpose are more enthusiastic, and will put more effort into pursuing their goals. So, effectively defining and communicating your organizational purpose and ensuring alignment to it is key to creating a motivated base of colleagues.

Your people should see purpose at every level of what they do, from tangible expressed statements such as the company's vision, mission and goals through to regular company communications and the type of language it uses. Ensuring alignment is about hiring the right people, which we'll talk about a bit later. Suffice to say, at this stage it's imperative that you hire people who understand your organizational purpose and have a natural affinity to it. It also means every job description for the organization should be linked to that purpose so everyone knows how they're contributing to success in achieving the company's purpose.

When people don't feel a sense of purpose, they lose motivation and become unenthusiastic about their job and the company. In the best case, they'll leave. In the worst case, they'll undermine the company culture through indifference and negativity.

You should never assume your people understand the purpose of the company and their role. Ensuring that it's broached in your regular annual review cycle is critical.

4. Empowered people

Even if your people understand your purpose and are aligned to it, it will amount to nothing unless they're empowered to contribute to it. In other words, they have the tools, control and authority to do their job. It can also mean they have the confidence to offer suggestions into how the organization functions, and how those they work with can do better.

Key habits to empower your employees include:

- Demonstrating your trust in their decision making
- Allowing them to make mistakes and treat them as opportunities to learn

- Asking guiding questions to engage and provide direction
- Demonstrating positive thinking and a focus on mutual problem-solving

Of course, there has to be a balance between empowering people and having a structure that delineates roles and provides checks and balances. This is important to avoid people telling others how to do their job, which will lead to conflict.

It's also important to follow best practice and avoid relying on individuals. Instead, emphasize that engaging with and harnessing the power of teams is the best way to achieve success.

5. Supported people feel enabled

Supporting an employee means ensuring they have the tools and resources they need to do their job. A person can be motivated by purpose and empowered to do their job. But without the right resources and tools to achieve their goals, they'll ultimately fail through lack of enablement.

This is the worst kind of failure because you set every other aspect of their role correctly and then fail at the last hurdle to support their success.

Here's how to ensure your people are supported in achieving their purpose:

- Ask them, "Do you have everything you need to do your job? Is there anything we can help you with?"
- Throughout the review cycle, make sure they think about what they need to do their job and identify any gaps.
- Provide a generous budget for learning and professional development so they can fill any gaps identified.
- Keep an eye on people working excessive hours or showing signs of stress. It may mean they're not sufficiently supported and are trying to do the right thing by filling gaps themselves. People cannot sustain this over a long period.

- Get people to think about where things will be over the short, medium and long term After all, you're in a growth company and things are going to change. If your people are always thinking in the present, they're not making preparations to ensure they have the right support for a larger, more demanding future.

You need to feel supported too. Ask yourself these same questions and determine whether you have the right team to succeed. If you don't, then do something about it.

6. They're happy, and enjoy what they do

People can feel the 'vibe' of a company the moment they walk in the door. Some places are serious and reserved, while others are vibrant and fun. But successful businesses share one thing in common: employees who are happy and enjoy what they do.

We believe happiness at work arises from a sense of purpose, empowerment and enablement. But people also have to like the work they're doing. It needs to be stimulating, interesting and motivating. If they don't enjoy what they do, they'll become bored and go somewhere else.

Once again you must take the time to check whether people still find their role interesting. If they don't, identify stretch opportunities to find more interesting work that suits their interests and needs.

Another suggestion is to give your people, particularly new and younger people, the opportunity to work across different areas of your business. People tend to gravitate towards what interests them. Don't be afraid to let people change roles, or move into new areas if the old one isn't working out. Non-performance in a role is often a sign of being in the wrong job rather than being incompetent.

As your organization grows, new jobs will open up. Encourage people to consider these new jobs, and even apply if they're interested.

Growth Pillar 3: Capability
What is capability?

Put simply, capability is the ability to get things done – individually and organizationally.

Individual capability includes the 'hard' and 'soft' skills your people have that allow them to do their job.

1. **Soft skills** are largely to do with emotion and interpersonal relationships. Strong soft skills lead to good decision-making and strong group cohesion. Soft skills should never be undervalued, particularly in people who manage your people and work with your suppliers and customers.

   A key benefit to having strong soft skills is the ability to deal with ambiguity and uncertainty. The importance of this skill should be obvious in a company where things are done without a recipe book and where every day can bring something new. Soft skills can be more difficult to define, measure and develop than hard skills. But that doesn't mean they're not real or important.

2. **Hard skills** can be thought of as competencies or technical 'know-how' in a specific knowledge domain (e.g. having the aptitude to design a machine or service a printer). And they can be taught to anyone with the right aptitude.

   Your company supports hard skills through its processes, documentation, training and IP assets. While hard skills can be grown internally, they can also be hired externally. This is useful if you need to develop skills in the company that you know exist elsewhere. Hard skills also tangibly prove your points of difference in the market.

   The intersection between soft and hard skills is where your business can really shine—a team of committed and effective individuals with a dynamic and powerful combination of soft and hard skills working together. This involves identifying talent and developing it from within, or hiring externally to develop your skill-base in line with your growing business.

But if you get it wrong, your people will feel unsupported and overworked, which can lead to attrition. You need to forecast demand and identify the need for specific skills in advance so you can deliver what your client needs.

Aside from people capabilities, successful growth in a B2B SME needs supporting organizational capabilities, such as processes, assets and resources that define what you do and how your people can deliver to your purpose.

Capabilities in successful growth B2B SMEs

Successfully growing B2B SMEs enable people with hard and/or soft skills by developing strong organizational capabilities.

1. Effective and regular communications

If you can't reach out to your people and engage with them, you can't motivate them and keep them aligned to company goals. Managers should cascade key communications from the leadership group to their teams. But when things get busy, it can drop off the team meeting agenda. So you need to develop and use company-level communications channels, particularly as your organization grows with more teams at more levels. Poor ongoing communication will lead to employees losing purpose, a loss of group cohesion, and a sense of isolation from the group.

Effective communication channels can include:

- developing a company intranet
- regular group emails from founder to staff
- regular face-to-face meetings
- weekly huddles
- offsite events or conferences where you can mingle and get face time with your people.

You also have the opportunity to join different team meetings as a 'surprise visitor'.

2. Strong reward and recognition

'Reward' generally means monetary rewards, and can include:

- fixed remuneration
- variable remuneration (e.g. bonuses)
- allocation of shares or options in the company.

Recognition means peer acknowledgement of individuals or teams, and is often undervalued as a way to motivate and increase job happiness. A few words of thanks and appreciation can make a massive difference, particularly as the company grows and your founding employees find themselves among a deeper pool of people. Two easy ways to drive recognition are:

- sending an end-of-month company email celebrating success
- regular award ceremonies for people who do great things.

Research into millennials (who will make up 75% of the workforce by 2025) suggest they're more strongly motivated by purpose than remuneration[44].

3. Embedded review process

For really small startups, it's common for the review process to be an informal and open catch-up over a coffee or beer. This is a valid and often effective way to ensure your people are in for the ride.

Unfortunately, this intimate and personal approach to reviews and appraisals doesn't scale well. It's a great way to maintain strong and trusting relationships with your inner core of leaders, but when your company grows beyond a dozen people it just becomes impractical.

Most people want to be able to track their progress in a structured and methodical way.

You need tools to assess the performance of your people and to identify any talent development opportunities. There should be a company-wide skills matrix (showing the hard and soft skills necessary to each staff member) that you can use as an assessment tool. It can also give you the raw material to write great job descriptions.

This is the foundation of assessing people against a known set of expectations, which is at the heart of fairness. When people feel their assessment is fair and objective, managers have license to provide more insightful and challenging feedback. But if roles aren't properly described, it's almost impossible to judge the effectiveness of an individual.

In our experience, the best form of assessment is for individuals to rate themselves on how well they delivered personal and professional goals. Getting people to rate themselves is a great way to encourage self-reflection and develop personal responsibility. The outcome is a shared commitment from the manager and team member to achieve agreed goals in an agreed timeframe.

4. Learning and development

With your skills matrix in place, and a process for ensuring people have the right skills to perform their jobs, you now have the ingredients to identify gaps that need to be bridged to enable great performance.

To succeed in this space you need to be serious about employees investing time and money in their personal learning and development. In a time-constrained environment it's easy for people to defer investing time in themselves. But in a growth company it's a false economy. As the company grows, the demands on skills and capabilities will also grow, so you need your people to develop themselves.

Later in this chapter we'll look at how growth affects individuals. But at this stage you just need to know that people who aren't motivated to grow personally and professionally in a growing company probably won't contribute much to that growth.

The good news is there's a wealth of high-quality learning and development resources available at moderate cost. Formal structured education is no longer the baseline requirement for professional development. Massive online open courses (MOOCs) provide almost unlimited opportunities for professional development. YouTube is the university of the future.

Along with external training, we recommend doing regular internal training and information-sharing through events such as 'lunch and learn' and 'brown bag' meetings. Giving your highly competent people the opportunity to present their learnings and knowledge to colleagues is a priceless way to share knowledge among your people while simultaneously giving positive recognition to the presenter for their effort.

5. Living documentation process

Documentation is the process organizations should follow to formalize knowledge and capability into procedures and instructions. Sadly, as with practically every focus area in this chapter, lack of time often undermines the documentation process.

But poor documentation can create considerable risks for your organization, including:

- excessive reliance on individuals and exposure to their loss through attrition
- the inability to understand the intersection of complex processes and identify opportunities to innovate your processes
- inefficient onboarding and training, leading to loss of productivity
- a sense of chaos among employees and over-reliance on others to get things done, which creates cultural silos.

Strong documentation processes ensure the critical capabilities of your company aren't being carried around inside people's heads. Here's how to establish good documentation processes:

- Have a central repository to create and store processes. Consider using online process-mapping software on a platform such as Confluence, or even just shared documentation in a formal structure.

- Ensure people get into the habit of documenting as they go. If you have to move too fast to keep adequate records, make sure people understand the need to circle back and fill in the necessary documentation later on.
- Consider adopting a formal quality-control process, such as ISO. These programs can be costly in terms of auditing, but they can also unlock access to clients and contracts where quality accreditation is a formal requirement.
- Hire people with technical writing skills.

It's also worth pointing out that if you ever get to a cash out scenario, your 'trade secrets' are more valuable if they're documented and retained.

Understanding time as an enabler for innovation

One of the great truisms of working life is that to be creative (the bedrock of innovation), people need time to reflect on how things are so they can then start thinking about how things can be.

But in the modern working life, time is in short supply. When teams are running to full capacity, spending every moment keeping up with orders, delivering client needs and bouncing around meeting requirements, it's impossible to reflect on what can be done better.

Unfortunately, growing companies face the greatest time pressures. People are frequently being stretched to cover additional work produced by that growth until new hires can be brought in to pick up the new work.

The *Listen, Innovate, Grow* framework is sequential. You start by listening to 'you', the market and customers, then start innovating (which includes defining priorities) and building on customer needs, and then consciously and continuously re-engineering your business to facilitate growth.

This is on top of your company's 'business as usual' operations where people spend most of their time delivering on the everyday requests and requirements of your customer base.

The critical success factor for innovation is giving your people enough time to be successful at each stage of the journey. This means investing in resources so the people in your business driving the innovation plan have enough time to reflect, think, create, build and plan within the LIG framework.

Here are some suggestions on how to facilitate this:

- Tell your team they should spend time 'outside' what they do every day to look at it as if they were an impartial observer.

- Encourage people to spend time on process innovation. Explain how investment their time in the short term will result in long-term time benefits due to increased efficiency.

- Support your team by factoring in thinking time in your overall human resourcing strategy. While it's tempting to run a lean team that operates around the clock to deliver, in reality it's the worst thing you can do to stifle and subvert innovation as your growth engine.

- Encourage everyone to take time out from the business – physically and mentally – to reinvigorate their thinking. It's amazing how the unconscious mind works on problems while the conscious mind is redirected by relaxing and pleasurable activities such as spending time alone or with family.

- Make innovation part of everyone's job role descriptions, and recognize and reward their success.

- Ensure people have the best equipment they need to do their jobs. Invest in quality computers, monitors and specialized equipment or software to save them time and magnify their effectiveness. Consider such spending as an investment in your people rather than a depreciable asset.

- Invest in training and development, and don't be afraid to let people train themselves in areas tangentially relevant to what they do. Developing expertise in a discipline not directly related to your job role can be a trigger for innovative thinking.

Organizational changes from growth and change management

In the first part of this chapter we looked at the people-driven success factors of growth, and gave you a range of ideas on how to make your people a success factor in your growth.

The second part of this chapter is about how your organization will change due to that growth. You'll learn what to expect as you grow, and how these effects can undermine your success. By being prepared, you can put strategies in place to mitigate the worst of these effects.

The effects of growth are broken into two areas:

1. Organizational elements affected by growth
2. People elements affected by growth.

Organizational elements affected by growth

Organizational elements, are the capabilities we reviewed in the previous section on supporting people that are delivered by the organization itself. Primarily, this includes employee experiences of the work environment, work culture and job roles. Some of these might seem obvious, but they can present serious issues for you and get in the way of you achieving your growth goals.

Changes to the work environment

It's safe to assume that a growing organization will take on more people. More people means you need more physical space. Sooner or later you'll outgrow your premises and need to find more spacious accommodation. But until that happens you'll probably have too many people squashed into an unreasonably small space.

This can lead to occupational health and safety issues and negative cultural impacts. People in confined spaces need to contend with more noise, disruption and lack of personal space. It can even create a sense of being in a 'happening' space where things are going fast, just as being in an empty office can create a sense of vacuum and lifelessness.

Both effects can be magnified by modern open-plan office environments. When space is limited and people are packed on top of each other in an open area, it can lead to more conflict, lower productivity and higher staff turnover. Solutions include making the decision to move earlier, 'hot desking' and encouraging people to work from home.

Another option is to rent a shared workspace such as WeWork—the go-to solution for professional services companies. The benefits of shared workspaces include:

- no long-term leases
- high-quality shared facilities
- the positive energy that can be found by co-locating with a bunch of other innovative and growing businesses.

On the downside, you'll probably spend more per square meter on occupancy and have to put up with other people's mess in the kitchen.

Most companies eventually end up in their own space, where they can put their own stamp on things.

Organizational structure

A major cause of *growth plateaus* is when a business with a relatively low headcount puts in an organizational structure that's inadequate for managing the needs of a larger business.

When a business outgrows a role, it gets split into smaller roles. New specialist managers and layers of management are then needed to maintain structure and coherent operations with a large group delivering in a more complex environment.

This brings both opportunities and risks. The opportunities come from being able to offer people more challenging roles with personal and professional growth opportunities. The risks come from people not being able to keep pace, or not having the desire or motivation to do so.

At the end of the day, you need to be careful. Learn about each person's appetite for challenge, growth and change, and decide whether they'll respond well to growing with the company, or whether the company can grow around them and leave them to do what they do best.

Changes to the work culture

As the employee base expands and the business changes, there will be impacts on the culture of your company. This needs to be observed and monitored to ensure you end up working in the company you want and that supports growth. Areas you need to pay particular attention to include:

- **Work-life balance:** Make sure there's balance between discretionary effort and avoidance of becoming a sweatshop. Be particularly wary of workaholics (including you) who create a feeling that the best way to get ahead is to work ridiculous hours. This isn't a positive scenario.

- **Politics:** Once an organization gets to around 20–30 people, the group dynamic changes and there's a tendency for politics to enter the workplace. People form coalitions, selectively share information, and make strategies to get ahead at the expense of their colleagues. This can lead to the balance in your company being lost as we described earlier.

- **Performance management:** Eventually you'll find yourself with an employee who isn't meeting expectations. It often happens when people are in the wrong role. But it can also happen when people are in the wrong company.
  Provide individuals with every opportunity to address any deficiencies in their role. But don't hesitate to manage out (i.e.

remove) people who damage the wellbeing and positive focus in the workplace through politics or other negative behaviors.

- **Inclusiveness:** As you get larger, it's easy to create two classes of employees—those on the inner and those on the outer. This can arise from naturally gravitating towards employees with high levels of motivation and energy, or who are star performers.

  But don't forget that every company also needs 'solid citizens'— people who do their job well but will never be brilliant or change the world. These people need to feel they're contributing as part of the team. Many people are also introverts who won't naturally join a conversation or make their ideas heard. Ironically, these people often have the best ideas because they spend more time listening and observing.

- **Innovation focus:** As more people join the organization, the sense of innovation can be lost as people begin seeing their role in the company as where they sit and what they do, rather than being creative. Many of the ideas in the 'listen' and 'innovate' sections of this book are designed to avoid this scenario.

New structural and support mechanisms for employees

Invest in people co-ordination and integration functions

Just like every other facet of the business, the way HR works in your firm will change as you bring in more people. At some point you'll need to create a specialist function that just deals with people. You'll also need to create new support mechanisms that provide for their needs in a more complex and diverse work environment.

Unfortunately, many growing organizations leave the decision to bring in a specialist HR function too late. It costs a lot of money, and doesn't seem to have a direct impact on your customers. There are always other more urgent things to invest in to increase capability, market your company better or drive new avenues to growth.

But delaying the decision to create a company capability to focus on employees can be an expensive mistake. Potential issues include:

- **Poor hiring decisions** that lead to attrition and instability, as well as lost investment in training and onboarding. It typically takes employees at least six months to become fully capable in their role, so bad hires can cost you big time.

- **Loss of good employees** you would rather keep because they don't feel motivated or supported in their roles.

- **People being left in the wrong roles** because you have no clear succession planning or career pathways. One of great things about growing is you can actually start offering people career progression. You need to let people grow with the firm and have the opportunity to explore alternative roles.

- **Low morale and disgruntlement** will occur if you don't get the basics right, such as:

  - setting up regular reviews
  - ensuring people are being paid at market rates for their roles
  - supporting staff with training and professional development
  - acknowledging staff regularly for the work they do.

Have strong processes to find and embed new talent

When you run a small company, onboarding a new employee is easy and quite unstructured. But as your company grows, and the number of roles in the business becomes more diffuse, you need to establish and develop a formal hiring and onboarding process. This can include:

- Developing incentives for your people to help you find and recruit other people

- Identifying applicant traits that fit your company culture, and establishing red flags that indicate a potentially poor fit in terms of culture or motivation

- Setting up a formal onboarding process, including first-day induction and procedures to ensure the new employee comes up to speed in their role and the general business as quickly as possible. Consider each hire as an opportunity to learn. If you're hiring good people for the right roles, they should have their own fertile spring of ideas. Rather than telling them what to do and how to do it, you should take the opportunity to see your business through their fresh eyes, and encourage them to speak up about any ideas or observations they make in these early days.

- A formal and scheduled review process (typically three months and six months from when they first join) to assess progress and ensure you're both satisfied that the relationship is progressing as desired. At these key check-in points you should be assessing progress and identifying any opportunities to address deficiencies or misunderstandings.

Have a formal exit review process

Despite your best efforts, sooner or later you'll lose people you'd rather keep in the business. This can happen for a variety of reasons, including career change goals, loss to competitors or loss of motivation.

It's important to learn from every employee who decides to leave your company. The best way to do this is to set up a formal exit interview process where you can explore and capture their motivations for leaving. This will help you identify common themes or issues leading to attrition.

Develop systems and processes to enable people

As you take on new people and grow, the business needs to scale up its support processes to keep people feeling supported and performing at their best over the long haul. Some basic steps you can take to deliver this include:

- **Having a staff intranet** that can be used to communicate, recognize and support employees. This will allow you to move away from mass emails to a more efficient and engaging media.

An intranet platform with a good content management system (CMS) will include features to:

- upload documents (including processes and training materials)
- manage organizational changes
- host company discussions
- broadcast company communications.

- **Developing day-to-day support processes**, including processes for managing expense claims, leave entitlements and induction documents. If these aren't properly managed and formalized as the company grows, it can lead to conflict and chaos.

- **Developing policies and procedures**. Every organization has different rules around pay reviews, professional and personal development, and training remuneration. They can be easily managed in a workplace with fewer than a dozen people, but in a workplace with more people, they become a full-time job. Having an expert consciously focusing on these time-consuming activities will ensure the founders spend their time focusing on business development and strategic growth opportunities.

- **Having individual training budgets**. A great way to encourage individual autonomy is to give each employee a set training budget (e.g. $2,000 per annum) and have them develop their own training plan that's aligned to the company mission. By doing this you give them scope to develop their own expertise to support the company goals. It's amazing how people can find creative learning opportunities that support your company in unexpected ways. It's also an opportunity to learn what they find interesting and develop a plan to put them in the right role to support the company growth strategy.

Changes to job roles

This concept is **fundamentally** important, and needs to be understood and carefully monitored as your business grows. There are two key effects:

1. **Businesses outgrow roles.** Some of the roles you created for your small business with four people almost certainly won't be needed in your business of 30 people. Over time you'll need to redefine, change and restructure roles, which will affect the people in those roles.

   For example, if you created a role in your small business to manage production, the scope of that role won't be the same when production increases by 8,000%.

   Another typical example is that when you have only a few people, the sales process is fundamentally different compared to when you have a hundred people. The first involves a sales person leading a small team of sales people, while the second involves developing a head of sales manager who facilitates sales through a team of sales people.

   The danger is that the people in those roles at the start of the journey shouldn't be in the new roles that are needed. Assuming they are, and just promoting them internally by rote, is dangerous.

2. **Roles outgrow people.** Similarly, while some roles grow with the business, the person in those roles may not grow with the role. In a growth company, small-scale methods and approaches need to change from being delivered by a subject matter expert to being delivered by a manager who can design and build a process.

   Unfortunately, the people who excel at doing things themselves with cleverness and ingenuity may not be good at managing others or creating strong processes. They may even become a growth constraint and a bottleneck. People can only do so much, and we've seen employees in this situation end up leaving their employer due to feeling overworked. However, the reality is often that they can't transform their job into a strong process that can scale up with the business, or delegate their increasing accountabilities to an employee team.

Businesses that outgrow roles may need an organizational change and a restructure. But when roles start outgrowing people you need to review the roles people are in and decide whether they should:

- stay in the current role
- be moved into a new role
- be removed from the company.

This can be unpleasant for everyone concerned.

Watch out: The Peter Principal

This is a good segue into reviewing individual capability limits.

You may be familiar with the concept of The Peter Principle (developed by educator Laurence J. Peters) that says people will generally be promoted on performance in current roles, meaning they'll ultimately be promoted to a position of incompetency.

In a growing company, this concept applies in reverse. Because roles grow and change, an employee in a growing company will remain capable in their role until it changes so much that they can no longer do it with their current skills and competency.

Of course, this won't always be the case. Many people are talented, motivated and capable of grow withing their roles. But sadly, action is sometimes needed to address the situation.

To manage the situation, we recommend continuously reviewing job fit as part of employee reviews (at least every six months) and, where required, taking remedial action such as training or even re-assignment.

Chapter summary

As SME organizations grow through the stages we discussed earlier, the only thing that will remain constant is change. Growth entails continual reappraisal of your leadership, company culture and people capability. And if you don't make the necessary changes you will inhibit your success.

You need to:

- Acknowledge change and acclimatize the workforce for disruption and growth
- Apply formal change-management principles to the business.

This being the case, you need to find an equilibrium between the benefits of stability (particularly efficiency) and the benefits of disruption (particularly innovation). As you grow, the balance will naturally shift towards stability and inertia, and away from innovation and agility.

You'll need to actively manage the business to ensure a degree of instability that encourages your people to continually reexamine and reassess how they do things.

The good news is the art of **listening and innovating** actually provides the formula to get the balance right. By listening to your customers you can identify where you need to disrupt through innovation because you're solving a demonstrable problem with an existing need.

Take action now

1. Get 360-degree feedback from your team on your leadership.
2. Develop a team of leaders to support you, and put them through the same process.
3. Develop a formal employee review process.
4. Develop a strong hiring process that includes references to soft and hard skills.
5. Develop support structures that allow your employees to contribute to growth.
6. Allocate individual training budgets to your people to give them autonomy on how they spend their budget in support of company goals.

CONCLUSION

We've given you a rich and detailed body of information, concepts, challenges, considerations and approaches to help you grow your startup or SME through B2B markets.

But in case your head is spinning, or you're suffering from information overload, we'll quickly recap the key topics we discussed in this book.

Keep in mind that our underlying premise is that the key to being successful in B2B markets and growing your startup or SME is to use our structured approach—the **Listen, Innovate, Grow B2B Framework.**

Listen

Listening occurs on three levels. We began with **listening to you** in Chapter 1, which is about understanding the vision, mission and goals both for you personally as an owner or manager and for your company. Listening to you is also about understanding your company's key strengths, capabilities and overall performance.

In Chapter 2, we talked about **listening to the market**, which means understanding the trends, characteristics and competitors within the industries and geographic markets you currently operate in, and those you wish to pursue moving forward.

The third type of listening, **listening to customers**, was discussed in Chapter 3. Listening to customers is about understanding the needs, objectives, priorities, motivations and buying behaviors of both your current and prospective customers. We also identified the different stakeholders within a B2B company you should take into consideration and developing an understanding of. And we identified and discussed four key methods to gain a deep understanding of these stakeholders.

Overall, the aim of listening is to know where the company should focus.

Innovate

We began Chapter 4 by identifying what you should look for in the three listening levels to best identify innovation opportunities.

In Chapter 5 we defined what business innovation is, and the ways it can be done. We also discussed the impact of executing multiple forms of business innovation on SME business growth.

In Chapter 6 we explained how the five types of innovations (product, service, process, organizational and marketing) can be applied in a B2B SME context.

We then discussed how to create your B2B company strategy in Chapter 7. The strategy you choose for your startup or SME is based on making choices about:

- where to focus (which is determined by listening)
- how to win by applying the five types of business innovation.

We concluded this section in Chapter 8 by explaining how to execute strategy, including how to:

- identify and manage key B2B customers and prospects
- prioritize, execute and manage the business innovations your company will undertake
- review and update your company's B2B strategies.

Grow

We began the section in Chapter 9 by discussing the four pathways to growth—*growing your overall market, increasing market share, price increases and extensions.*

In Chapter 10 we discussed how to manage growth by examining the four stages of growth—*starting up, forming, spreading and corporatization,* along with their key characteristics and what you should do in each stage.

In Chapter 11 we discussed how to manage your company's finances as it innovates and grows. We discussed the importance of managing key aspects such as costs, overheads, cash flows, billing and payment cycles, as well as the need to increase your vigilance of financial management as your company scales and grows.

Finally, in Chapter 12 we talked about managing your most important asset—your people. We looked at the three pillars of organizational growth—leadership, culture and capabilities. We then examined the change elements that occur in your company as it grows, how such changes affect each of the three pillars, and what steps you can take to ensure your company has a positive environment, innovation and growth.

Where to from here?

Hopefully we've demonstrated that by applying the concepts and approaches of the **Listen, Innovate, Grow B2B Framework**, startups and SMEs can take advantage of the significant opportunities B2B markets present. By sharing the experiences and journeys of various SMEs, we've tried to show you what success through the adoption of the LIG B2B framework looks like. But as you may have experienced with other business endeavors, success doesn't come easily, and you will have your fair share of challenges.

Don't let the challenges of operating a B2B SME dissuade you from giving it your all to achieve success. There is so much potential.

Revisit and reflect on the concepts and approaches we've presented to you. Discuss them with your partners, colleagues, employees, business advisors or Board.

The world of business is fast moving and forever changing, and your competitors aren't sitting idly by. So, start now!

Take small steps if necessary. Apply one or two of the approaches we've discussed. You can incorporate more as you feel more confident and have the resources and capacity to do so.

The growth journey is a long one, with plenty of ups and downs. But as Empower Construction and many others in our tribe are experiencing, the journey can be a positive one that gives you and your team a sense of achievement, fulfillment and happiness.

Good luck!

Michael and Garreth.

Continue to listen, innovate and grow

This book introduced you to concepts and approaches that can help you and your company on your B2B growth journey. To help you apply these approaches, visit **listeninnovategrow.com** for templates, checklists and videos that will further demonstrate these concepts, and help you:

- understand B2B customers
- plan and execute your innovation initiatives, B2B strategies and customer plans
- manage your company's growth.

CASE STUDIES

CASE STUDY 1

Connective

Who we spoke with

Mark Heron, Director

About the business

Connective is a provider of the Mortgage Origination platform based in Melbourne, Australia. Connective entered the industry in 2003 with a new business model that was fairer to brokers and allowed them to keep more of their profit. Connective partners with brokers in open and transparent relationships. It collaborates with a wide variety of lenders, and operates in aggregation.

The Connective company journey

Connective started with three people in 2003 and now has over 100 employees. Connective has changed the face of mortgage broking in Australia and is now the leading mortgage broker in the country, with a large and growing base of brokers online.

How they applied the LIG framework

Book concept	What they did	Key learnings
Listen	Developed close trusting relationships with brokers. Focused on the most successful brokers to see what they did well. Maintained close involvement with industry events and regulatory bodies. Had their IT team listen to customers continuously to guide product development.	Understand excellence and what sets apart your best customers. Align to what they need. Listen to multiple channels – the market, customers and industry partners.
Innovate	Developed a new contractual structure that was more equitable and appealing to mortgage brokers. Allowed mortgage brokers to treat trailing commissions as an asset to trade and deal. Developed cloud-based mortgage broking platform with strong focus on application programming interfaces (APIs).	Understanding how customers perceive value unlocks strategies to gain market share by increasing their value. Listen to customer feedback about your product, and use it to guide decisions about where to invest in it. Move first, and take calculated risks based on your own assessment of market needs. Listening to customers means giving them what they want and need, not doing what they say.

Book concept	What they did	Key learnings
Grow	Finance: Focused on a 4–5-year horizon, kept costs low, and retained capital in the business by not taking dividends for owners. People: Owners maintained their hands-on approach throughout the journey. Built a team around them to deliver to their goals. Marketing: Used networking to quickly gain scale and market share. Corporatized: Developed strong processes aligned to their size.	Keep a long-term focus and build capability to scale up. Get the right people on board with the same energy and belief as the founders. Invest in people and the support structures that enable their success in your business.

What they found challenging

Getting the right people on board and retaining them.

Advice for other B2B SMEs

- Listen to understand customer needs, not just what they say.
- Be prepared to think beyond how things are now to how they should be.
- Always hire the best available person, even if it costs more.
- Develop a strong onboarding process.
- Act swiftly and decisively if you don't have the right team on board.

In their words

"Make sure you can think and plan for the business success over a 3–5-year journey, not just an initial 12 months."

"Be more 'Steve Jobs-ish' for want of better terminology – where you need to look around and you need to find things that people don't even know they need yet and how you can get that ahead of them to position the business."

"Be better at determining the talented people and wherever possible spend a bit more money and hire a better person... we actually hired better people to hire better people too."

"If you don't corporatize your business you will struggle going from a small to medium size business because lots of i's won't be dotted and t's crossed and all of a sudden you'll have so many problems, you know, it's just not worth it."

CASE STUDY 2

Intelledox

Who we spoke with

Michelle 'Chelle' Melbourne, Co-founder and Executive Director

About the business

Intelledox is an Australian IT company that helps its clients achieve digital transformation by automating business flows and customer journeys. Intelledox aims to be the global leader in digital transaction management software, with a footprint across financial services, insurance, government, education and health

The Intelledox company journey

Chelle founded Intelledox with her partner Phil, in 1991. Intelledox has now grown to a company with more than 70 people, with offices in Dallas, Texas, New York, Singapore, Sydney and global headquarters in Canberra, Australia. More than 140 global customers and millions of users trust the Intelledox Infiniti platform.

How they applied the LIG framework

Book concept	What they did	Key learnings
Listen	Relied on their business judgment and nous to respond to challenges and avoid pitfalls along the way. Reviewed why they had a low conversion from shortlisting to winning tenders with the largest corporates and government clients, and changed to a partner channel model.	'Listened' to feedback about what stopped them winning big projects, and created a new channel model that allowed them to partner with other businesses.
Innovate	Pushed themselves to meet the challenges of large government and private sector organizations to develop world-leading technology. Made a deliberate step away from IT consultancy to develop IP in their product that would enable repeatable concurrent revenue. Gained a strong appreciation of the human aspect of technology – not just building new products, but also supporting systems for customers to deliver a great experience.	Allowed 'extreme' customers to push them to develop a better product. Changed how they operate to create IP to automate process flows (i.e. product innovation). Identified that innovation isn't just about a better product. It's about changing how you operate to do things better, more efficiently and deliver a better customer experience (i.e. process innovation).

Book concept	What they did	Key learnings
Grow	Realized that their consultancy business wouldn't scale, so took on people and charged them out at a profit. Created structure and processes to support a larger business once they got to 25 employees. Hired a CEO to take their business to the next level of growth.	Identified themselves as going through growth stages, and reviewed and changed their structure to maintain their organizational ability to grow in line with their revenue growth.

What they found challenging

Moving through the stages of hiring people, and working out how to transform the business to function as an employer and organization.

Advice for other B2B SMEs

- Think on your feet. Learn from failure and adjust your approach to find success.
- Focus on culture and hiring people who love what they do.

In their words

"In business, we found that if you are playing in an ecosystem that is sophisticated and world class, particularly when you are building a piece of software, your software is going to be sophisticated and world class."

"People seek order, and they seek to know where they are in the system and what is expected of them. And that critical mass, I would suggest, around 20-30 people is where you have to start to have processes, procedures and policies."

"We have over-serviced our customers, we have loved them to death. So, we are hungry for their feedback. Whilst it has cost us a lot of money to over-service them, they have been very loyal, because our mutual success is what matters."

CASE STUDY 3

Ikabo

Who we spoke with

Cindy Lenferna De La Motte, Managing Director

About the business

Ikabo is a technology company that has a core product based on SaaS technology. The Ikabo Incubator leverages an online crowdsourcing platform to provide services related to innovation, customer and employee engagement, and strategic thinking

The Ikabo company journey

Ikabo started in September 2016, and Cindy has been the Managing Director since the company's inception. The team includes a Head of Innovation and a Head of Technology. All three have more than 15 years' experience working at large corporates and in B2B markets. As a result, Ikabo has adopted a very strategic approach in terms of building the business, product development and their go-to-market approach.

During the first six months of the company's inception, it was 'all hands on deck' to develop their strategy, marketing and brand positioning, create a minimal viable product (MVP) and secure some initial foundation clients.

Since then, the Ikabo team has been continually evolving its product and roadmap based on customer feedback and market trends, as well continuing to build its customer base. Ikabo operates mainly in Australia, but is pursuing leads in New Zealand and the United Kingdom. Ikabo works with large corporates, higher education institutions and government departments.

How they applied the LIG framework

Book concept	What they did	Key learnings
Listen	Conducted 30 in-depth interviews to understand the needs, challenges and problems of potential customers and confirmed the strategy developed. Conducted extensive competitor reviews to understand current technical and user features to inform sales and marketing approach to find their USP. Regularly conducted Strategic Customer Selling Meetings to understand customer requirements, challenges and issues. Feedback was given back to the team in debrief sessions.	Ongoing listening is critical to identifying opportunities and having a customer-driven strategy. Obtain feedback from both the buyers and users within your customers and prospects.

Book concept	What they did	Key learnings
Listen cont.	At the end of every client engagement, a review called the Customer Retrospective was conducted to ascertain what was learned, whether key success factors were met, and areas for improvement. Feedback was also incorporated into the market requirements document (see below) and product plans. The company created a Market Requirements Document—a "living document" with all market, competitor and customer information that is regularly updated and reviewed.	
Innovate	**Product Innovation:** Quarterly product development meetings were conducted to review activities and feedback from previous three months as well as look forward for the next three, six and nine months.	Identified themselves as going through growth stages, and reviewed and changed their structure to maintain their organizational ability to grow in line with their revenue growth.

Book concept	What they did	Key learnings
Innovate cont.	Product changes were made due evolving needs of clients. (Ikabo products are built on widely available open source technologies.) **Marketing Innovation:** The team developed personas for key buying group members (Decision-Makers, Influencers and Change Agents) to understand the buyers' journey, objectives and challenges to develop targeted messages and use the appropriate communication channels. Ikabo transitioned from focusing on foundational activities (such as creating a company website), collateral and product demos, to content marketing activities such as hosting breakfast events and using LinkedIn to drive thought leadership and business success stories.	Identifying a change agent can be difficult, but is often critical to getting B2B buyers to buy. Need to transition to marketing activities to gain visibility and brand awareness, and demonstrate expertise and thought leadership to "buyers" (ie. Decision-Makers, Influencers and Change Agents).

Book concept	What they did	Key learnings
Grow	Ran the business very lean. Currently, the Managing Director is the primary person for all business development activities. (Little additional funds for inbound or lead-generation activities.) Regarded people as their most important asset. Ikabo philosophy is to create a 'culture of safety and learning' where all team members can contribute, discuss, debate and ask tough questions, and are encouraged to try new ideas to move business forward.	Need to have some budget for business development activities to find more opportunities and generate more referrals.

Ambitions

- To build and grow a successful business that supports our clients to unlock the potential of their people to drive competitive advantage and increase productivity.
- To support our ecosystem and partners to be successful.
- To provide a dynamic and interesting workplace for my people to grow.

Challenges

- Limited funds inhibiting grand business development/marketing efforts.
- Identifying the change agent. They're not easy to identify, as it can be different (i.e. different title/function) every time.
- Organizations don't really know that some of their engagement and innovation problems can be solved through Ikabo technology.

Advice

- Take a structured approach to develop and validate your strategy.
- Have some funds for marketing for lead generation activities.
- Become resourceful.
- Ask for help.
- Try new ways.

Personal journey

Managing Director Cindy has grown a lot by overcoming challenges
"You really learn when you must do!"

In their words

"You need to experiment. The results will inspire you."

"Be more open to saying 'Yes'. Take a leap of faith."

"Surround yourself with good people for inspiration and support and guidance."

CASE STUDY 4

Bellissimo Law Group
Professional Corporation

Who we spoke with

Mario Bellissimo, Founder

About the business

The Bellissimo Law Group PC (BLG PC) is an immigration law firm that specializes in complex immigration appeals and inadmissibility cases for persons applying for permanent and temporary residence in Canada. In terms of a B2B context, BLG PC works with lawyers and consultants who have been assigned to deal with such matters.

The Bellisimo Law Group company journey

Mario Bellissimo started on his own with two associates who practiced in different areas in 1998 by providing services in many areas of law beyond Immigration Law, including Criminal Law, Employment Law, Real Estate, Corporate/Commercial and Family Law. In 2002, recognizing the market need, he repositioned the firm with a singular focus on Immigration, Citizenship and Refugee Law. Mario in particular began specializing in Immigration Litigation and Admissibility. Between 2005 and 2009, Mario won a number of high-profile cases that gave him significant media exposure. These legal victories were catalysts in driving the growth of BLG PC and positioning it today as one of Canada's leading immigration law specialists.

How they applied the LIG framework

Book concept	What they did	Key learnings
Listen	Conducted client audits at key touchpoints: initial consultation, six months and post-case completion. The aim of the audits was to look for trends, issues and identify where work was coming from. Attended events and seminars specific to immigration.	Listening is key to understanding client needs and areas of opportunity.
Innovate	**Marketing Innovation** In 2000, an initial marketing plan was developed and executed. The aim was to establish core foundation elements to serve many areas of law. 2005–2009: Engaged in thought leadership—publishing, speaking and teaching, as well as media activities (e.g. TV, newspaper).	Need to be consistent with marketing activities, as they can require a significant amount of time to have an impact. Taking a niche focus can be an effective strategy if you can identify the market opportunity and are willing to put in the necessary focus and investment to deliver such an offering.

Book concept	What they did	Key learnings
Innovate cont.	**Specialization** Changed core focus of BLG PC to working on Litigation/Admissibility cases on behalf of law firms and companies focusing on the most difficult areas of law such as multiple violations and misrepresentations. **Differentiation/Positioning** Positioned BLG PC to be a highly skilled, professional, top performing immigration firm. (As a result, acquired, retained and trained the very best and brightest people, very credible office address in classy office building, full business attire.)	Need to be consistent with marketing activities, as they can require a significant amount of time to have an impact. Taking a niche focus can be an effective strategy if you can identify the market opportunity and are willing to put in the necessary focus and investment to deliver such an offering.

Book concept	What they did	Key learnings
Grow	Focused strongly on staff. BLC PC gives them opportunities to grow by enabling them to participate in the legal community and become authors, speakers and develop policy. All staff are given a monetary allowance towards their professional development with training targets set each year. Heavy reinvestment to finance growth. Founding associated reinvested heavily for 15 years.	Strong focus on developing and engaging people is key to growing a business, especially when it is a knowledge-based industry and specialization is the core foundation of your business strategy.

Ambitions

BLG PC will continue working on high-level cases, expand its public relations and policy development role, and begin cultivating future leaders in the firm.

What they found challenging

The changing face of law. It's difficult to keep up with the legal changes due to the changing requirements in other areas such as Accounting, HR and Regulatory.

Advice for other B2B SMEs

1. Specialize

    - Like your specialty.
    - Make sure those around you share that like.

2. Your people

    - Hire the best and brightest, but make sure they have good people skills.
    - Make sure they have the same values as the rest of the team.
    - Develop your people, and give them opportunities to grow.

Personal Journey

Positives: The satisfaction from building the team.

Negatives: It was very challenging at the beginning of my career as some aspects of the legal system were not accessible, concentrated in the hands of a few stakeholders, and not as transparent. This was very difficult to overcome, and at times seemingly insurmountable. Thankfully we were successful and now as one of the larger participants, we remember our journey and hope to change that for others.

In their words

"You need to be a self-starter, wear multiple hats, have no ego and contribute to the collective."

CASE STUDY 5

Palladium Insurance

Who we spoke with

Sylvie Forget-Swim, Managing Partner

About the business

Palladium Insurance is an independent insurance brokerage offering auto, home, commercial, life and health insurance protection to clients across Canada.

The Palladium Insurance company journey

- In 1971, the firm Bourgeois Cote Forget was founded by Guy Forget, Gerry Cote, Eddie Cote and Raymond Bourgeois.
- In 1992, Palladium Insurance was started by Tim Snelling.
- 2005: Sylvie joined Bourgeois Cote Forget. The company was a cluster of two brokerages. Sylvie purchased the Bourgeois book of business and joined her father, Guy Forget as a partner. In 2007, Monique Oliver joined Bourgeois Cote Forget and purchased the Cote book of business as Gerry and Eddie retired.
- 2010: Cory Villeneuve became a partner with Sylvie when Guy Forget retired.

- 2013: Discussions commence about 'de-clustering' the business. Monique, Cory and Sylvie de-clustered and merged with Palladium to become partners with Tim Snelling.
- 2013 Formed Palladium Insurance Group.
  - A bilingual firm focusing on niche commercial markets in the Ottawa-Gatineau area.
  - Rationale: The management team believed there was an opportunity to deliver more value in the commercial space that was dominated by large, corporate firms.
- 2015: Greg Strahl became a partner.

How they applied the LIG framework

Book concept	What they did	Key learnings
Listen	Held annual policy review meetings with clients to review their business operations and plans. Hosted VIP hockey nights and invited selected clients. It was an opportunity to have informal discussions with key clients. All client feedback was kept in Word documents and shared at weekly staff meetings across all offices.	It's useful to have both formal and informal channels to capture customer feedback and insight.

Book concept	What they did	Key learnings
Innovate	**Marketing Innovation** In 2005, put a strong focus on advertising and branding. Key partnerships within the community (e.g. hockey rinks, baseball stadiums, the arts, Yellow Pages and newspapers) In 2016, expanded marketing activities to include LinkedIn, Twitter and blogs to educate and engage clients as well as conduct Facebook campaigns. These activities are now managed by an external agency. Tracked and reported on campaigns to understand their impact and effectiveness. **Product Innovation** Niche Offerings: Developed insurance products for specific industries—dental, funeral, brewers and construction. A holistic end-to-end solution: Niche offerings were used as the hook to capture all of the client's commercial and personal insurance needs.	Educating and informing clients is an important part of acquiring and retaining business customers. It's important to use multiple marketing tactics. Marketing is a key driver to business growth. Dedicating resourcing is required as your business continues to grow. Measurement and reporting are key to determining impact and understanding what tactics to use.

Book concept	What they did	Key learnings
Innovate cont.	**Service Innovation** "Concierge-style service": If clients wanted full service then it was just one phone call. Each niche product had an assigned lead/single point of contact. This person would then liaise with the appropriate people within the company.	
Grow	**Geographic expansion:** Expanded to offer niche products nationally. **Product enhancement:** Expanded coverage for policies (e.g. new privacy breach coverage for doctors. **Acquisitions:** Acquired smaller firms, many of which were microbusinesses. **People:** Encouraged and paid for staff development and accreditations (e.g. Certified Insurance Professional, Certified Risk Manager). Focused on hiring the right staff to meet client and company requirements.	

Ambitions

To be the trusted Canadian brokerage that focuses on customer service in a way that each individual client can receive their services the way they wish to receive them—online, in person or a combination of both

What they found challenging

- Getting the right people.
- Lack of accounting: made it hard to determine the value of the company's book of business.
- Merging data in Palladium systems.

Advice for other B2B SMEs

- Get the right staff.
- Use a formal strategic-planning process.
- Be flexible. The world is always changing.
- Admit when you have made a mistake, fix it and move on.

Personal Journey

Positives

- Exceeded expectation. The company now has five partners.
- Sylvie gets to work with the clients she loves.

Negatives:

- Can be a struggle to achieve work-life balance.

In their words

"Everyone is working in the niche areas they like. It's the perfect storm."

CASE STUDY 6

Empower Construction

Who we spoke with

Ryan Steyn, Founder and Managing Director and Julia Sampo, Marketing Director.

About the business

Empower Construction is an award-winning business that advises on and installs cladding for residential and multi-residential developers, commercial builders and architects. Empower's Founder and Managing Director, Ryan Steyn was awarded the 2017 Optus Young Business Leader of the Year.

The Empower Construction company journey

Empower was founded in 2007 by Ryan Steyn.

He started as a sub-contractor installing cladding.

In 2008, Ryan won his first contract to both supply and install cladding. He recognized that by purchasing his own materials and doing the installations himself, he could solve the problem of downtime labor that builders and other contractors were experiencing, not to mention provide a better offering.

In 2009, with a staff of ten, Ryan and his team worked in the residential space completing jobs for home builders/construction companies. By

2010, Empower had established themselves as the benchmark for external cladding in the residential construction space. They also worked with Metricon Homes, a tier-one residential builder in Australia and CSR Hebel, a product manufacturer, to pioneer the installation manual for residential cladding application.

Empower expanded in 2012/2013 to work with both residential and non-residential clients.

How they applied the LIG framework

Book concept	What they did	Key learnings
Listen	Conducted weekly site meetings on all projects. Conducted quarterly management meetings with key clients to discuss current issues and prevent future ones. Conducted builder's senior manager meetings where Ryan Steyn met with national/regional construction managers (i.e. the buyers) every six months to understand the clients' needs. Feedback was captured via Google Forms and Asana, and used to debrief all Empower staff at company meetings.	It's useful to have both formal and informal channels to capture customer feedback and insight.

Book concept	What they did	Key learnings
Listen cont.	All meetings were given an "Identify-Discuss-Solve" segment to discuss and resolve client issues. Ryan started talking to industry contacts such as builders/construction companies, suppliers and developers as well as reading Australian and international industry magazines to stay up-to-date on emerging trends and issues.	Understanding the needs, priorities and issues of buyers is critical. Understanding the trends, issues and approaches used in other markets helps to identify opportunities and meet client needs.
Innovate	**Product Innovation:** Client feedback led Empower to expand their offering to cladding, rendering and painting. **Marketing Innovation:** In 2008, the focus was on generating awareness and providing education about cladding through articles and case studies. By 2017, their marketing became very targeted, and was aimed at educated and engaging key decision-makers. This was achieved by providing content on LinkedIn and in *CEO Magazine*.	Client feedback can be a source of innovation opportunities. You need to change and expand your marketing strategy as your business grows and evolves to ensure both the content and channels used meet the needs of the decision-makers and influencers you are targeting.

Book concept	What they did	Key learnings
Innovate cont.	**Process Innovation:** Empower's management team recognized the need to know how to grow and measure whether they were growing. They implemented the Entrepreneurial Operating System (EOS), a structured approach for strategy development including quarterly and annual planning sessions, action plans, review and measurement.	
Grow	Developed a very strong emphasis on people. Hired and fired based on the core values of dedication, integrity, adaptability, teamwork and faith. Engaged in open dialogue in their quarterly meetings. Ryan Steyn focused heavily on identifying new opportunities, strategy and planning to grow the business.	Your team must share the same values, purpose and desire to grow. Alignment and engagement of staff are key to working together to drive growth. Growth requires a focused, planned approach.

Ambitions

Initially, Ryan wanted to have his own business and help people by giving them opportunities to learn, grow and better themselves. This is why he named the company 'Empower'.

Financially, Ryan's initial goal was to make $1 million in revenue. His goal for 2018 is to make $1 million in profits, which the company is on track to achieve.

The ten-year target for Empower is to make $100m in revenue and $10m in profit.

Advice for other B2B SMEs

- Make business decisions, not emotional ones.
- Hire slow, fire fast.
- Make sure your team wants to grow.
    - "They must get, want it, and be able to do it."—Julia Sampo, Marketing Director.
- Look at failures as lessons.
- Never underestimate the power of relationships.
- Know your purpose.
    - "Do it for a reason, not just for the money."—Ryan Steyn, founder.
- Constantly learn.
- Have faith.
    - "Believe in your purpose."
    - "Believe in your people."
    - "Believe in God."

Personal Journey

Positives

- Growing their people, developing their skills and seeing them grow.

Negatives:

- It can be tough to make decisions about people.

In their words

"Do more than what you are paid for, and you will eventually be paid for more than what you do."

APPENDIX

Innovation Checklist Matrix

The following checklist outlines some key criteria you should take into consideration when evaluating business innovation opportunities.

Criteria	'You'	The market	Customers
Alignment to goals and vision	Do the initiatives align with our agreed goals and vision?	Will they potentially serve the target markets we seek?	Will they meet the needs of our strategic customers and/or key target prospects?
Impact on company growth	Will it help us achieve our growth targets/aspirations? How does this compare to other initiatives? What trade-offs must be made?	Which markets will the initiative target? What are the size, growth, levels of competition and barriers to entry for those markets and industries being targeted with this innovation initiative?	Does this focus on high-growth/high-value customers? What growth can we expect from them? What's the impact on growth of our strategic customers and key accounts?

Customer impact	How can we best serve the customers affected? Are these the customers we seek?	What markets do we seek? Are they currently being served by competitors? If so, can we differentiate or disrupt?	Will the initiative meet the needs of current key strategic customers/key accounts? What's the expected impact (e.g. uptake, cross-sell, upsell)?

REFERENCES

....

Chapter 1

1. www.ge.com/ar2014/ceo-letter
2. www.microsoft.com/investor/reports/ar/3/financialreview/business description/index.html
3. www.sapintegratedreport.com/2013/en/strategy-and-business-model/vision-mission-and-strategy.html
4. www.citigroup.com/citi/about/mission-and-value-proposition.html

Chapter 2

5. www.evolveresearch.com
6. www.microsoft.com/investor/reports/ar/3/financialreview/business description/index.html
7. www.ge.com/ar2014/ceo-letter
8. "There's a S.M.A.R.T way to management's goals and objectives," Management Review AMA Forum 70 (11) 35-36
9. www.mckinsey.com/business-functions/strategy-and-corporate-finance/our-insights/enduring-ideas-the-three-horizons-of-growth
10. *Inside the Buyer's Brain*, by Lee Fredriksen, Elizabeth Harr, Sylvia Montgomery and Aaron Taylor, p.36, 2013

Chapter 3

11. "The New B2B Sales Imperative," *Harvard Business Review* by Nicholas Toman, Brent Adamson and Cristina Gomez, March-April 2017

12. *How and Why Large Companies Make Product Selections: You Know How to Sell, Now Learn How Companies Buy* by Brian Burns

13. *The Challenger Customer: Selling to the Hidden Influencer Who Can Multiply You Results* by Brent Adamson, Matthew Dixon, Pat Spenner and Nick Toman, p.145, 2015.

14. "How B2B Sales Can Benefit From Social Selling," *Harvard Business Review*, by Laurence Minky and Keith Quesenbery, November 2016.

Chapter 5

15. Unlocking Everyday Innovation, *CommBank Business Insights Report*, Commonwealth Bank of Australia, 2017.

16. "The 12 Different Ways for Companies to Innovate," *MIT Sloan Management Review* by Mohanbir Sawhney, Robert Wolcott and Inigo Arroniz, 2006.

17. "The 12 Different Ways for Companies to Innovate," *MIT Sloan Management Review* by Mohanbir Sawhney, Robert Wolcott and Inigo Arroniz, 2006.

18. Unlocking Everyday Innovation, *CommBank Business Insights Report*, Commonwealth Bank of Australia, 2017.

19. www.innovation-management.org/business-model-innovation

20. Unlocking Everyday Innovation, *CommBank Business Insights Report*, Commonwealth Bank of Australia, 2017.

21. In Full Focus: Insights into Business Confidence, DBM research, 2016.

22. In Full Focus: Insights into Business Confidence, DBM research, 2016.

23. Key Small Business Statistics, Statistics Canada, June 2016

24. *Exporting: A Key Driver of SME Growth and Profits,* by Business Development Corporation, April 2017.

25. www.silfab.ca

Chapter 6

26. *Lean Start Up: Adding a Key Step for B2B Innovation* by Dan Adams, Dave Loomis and Carol Adams, 2015

27. *The Oslo Manual*, www.oecd.org

28. Unlocking Everyday Innovation, *CommBank Business Insights Report*, Commonwealth Bank of Australia, 2017.

29. "Canada's Uniquely Co-operative Culture Is a Boom to Tech Innovation," *The Globe and Mail*, May 17, 2017.

30. OECD, Glossary of Statistical Terms, stats.oecd.rg

31. 2017 High Growth Firms Study by Hinge Consulting

32. *CXcellence: How to achieve CX in B2B by B2B Marketing (UK)*, 2017

33. *CXcellence: How to achieve CX in B2B by B2B Marketing (UK)*, 2017

34. *What You Should Know About B2B Referrals But Probably Don't* by Influitive and Heinz Marketing, 2017.

35. *What You Should Know About B2B Referrals But Probably Don't* by Influitive and Heinz Marketing, 2017.

36. *What You Should Know About B2B Referrals But Probably Don't* by Influitive and Heinz Marketing, 2017.

37. *The B2B Executive Playbook* by Sean Geehan, 2011

38. *The Messenger is the Message* by Mark Organ and Deena Zenyk, 2017

39. *Make Your Mark with Influencer Marketing* by Tendo Communications, 2017

Chapter 7

40. *Playing to Win: How Strategy Really Works* by A.G Lafley and Roger Martin, 2013

41. *Stuck in the Middle: Mid-sized Enterprises in Australia Presentation* by the Department of Industry, Innovation and Science, 2017

42. *SMEs and Growth: Challenges and Winning Strategies*, CDC, October 2015.

Chapter 8

43. *Rain Group, 5 Keys to Maximizing Sales* by Mike Schultz and John Doerr

44. *Rain Group, 5 Keys to Maximizing Sales* by Mike Schultz and John Doerr

Chapter 9

45. *Marketing Myopia*, by Theodore Levitt, Best of HBR, 1960.

Chapter 12

46. "Do You Have the Right Leaders for Your Growth Strategies?" *McKinsey Quarterly* by Katherine Herrmann, Asmus Komm and Sven Smit, July 2011.

47. "Workforce 2020: What You Need to Know Now," *Forbes*, May 2016.

ACKNOWLEDGEMENTS

Thank you to our fellow startup and SME owners and managers for buying *Listen Innovate Grow* and reading this far. We appreciate that you are all extremely busy. It has been privilege to write this book for you. We hope it helps you achieve both your personal and professional ambitions. Please email us at info@listeninnovategrow.com to let us know how you are implementing the ideas and approaches to work in your business.

We would also like to thank the entrepreneurs and companies who gave up their valuable time to contribute to the case studies and examples in this book: Mario Bellissimo, Cindy Lenferna de la Motte, Julia Sampo, Ryan Steyn, Sylvie Forget-Swim, Chelle Melbourne and Mark Heron. You are all great examples of the success that startups and SMEs can have in B2B.

This book would never have been completed without our design and editing team. Thank you to Ikmah (aka "Wildeagles 99") at 99Designs for the book cover design. It really reflects the non-corporate, practical and action-oriented look and feel we were keen to convey. Thank you to Bill Harper for the line editing and Louisa Deasey for proof reading.

A very special thank you to Kelly Exeter. Kelly, you truly understood the vision and aim of *Listen Innovate Grow*. Your structural editing and book interior design has raised the quality of this book to its highest potential.

Thanks also to our marketing team at Ginger Ninjas – Tim, Corinne and Dan – for creating the website and supporting resources to accompany this book. Your advice, input and support has helped to make *Listen Innovate Grow* a truly actionable resource for our fellow B2B Start Ups and SMEs.

We would also like to thank our friends and family for their unwavering support, encouragement, patience and assistance throughout this journey.

Special thanks to Darren, Michelle, Kim, Paulina, Cindy, Melanie, Donna, Kate and Shane.

Without you all, we ourselves would not have been able to Listen Innovate and Grow.

Michael and Garreth

www.ingramcontent.com/pod-product-compliance
Lightning Source LLC
Chambersburg PA
CBHW061628220326
41598CB00026BA/3922